THE BUSINESS OF DINING

A Guide to Making
a Five-Star Impression

★★★★★

DEBBIE VON AHRENS

The Three Tomatoes Book Publishing

Published October 2023
ISBN: 979-8-9884613-9-5
Library of Congress Control Number: 2023917911

For information address:
The Three Tomatoes Book Publishing
6 Soundview Rd.
Glen Cove, NY 11542

Cover and interior design: Susan Herbst
Author Photo: ©2023 Bob Sacha
Illustrations: ©2023 woolypear

Advance Praise for
The Business of Dining:
A Guide to Making a Five-Star Impression

"The *Business of Dining* is a must-have addition to anyone's library, whether you go out to eat for a living or just want to enhance your own experience. Debbie has written a thorough hosting/ dining primer on all you need to know, literally from soup to nuts (or cheese), including which fork to use, how to pronounce a food, read a wine label, use and fold your napkin and so much more. I would buy this book for every person in management, any sales force or entertaining position. I'd also buy this book for any waitstaff looking to up their game. There isn't an adult who couldn't benefit from the tips in this book!"

~ Joanne Cini, former SVP Sales and Marketing
NBC Television Stations

"I've been selling luxury real estate in New York City for 20+ years and dining out with clients is an aspect of my work I truly enjoy— trying many restaurants and cuisines is a great passion of mine. Notwithstanding my years of experience in this regard, this book offered insightful tips and helpful reminders. An outstanding primer for a young professional and an excellent refresher for all who enjoy fine dining and appreciate proper etiquette. A quick and fun read!"

~ Cathy Taub, Senior Global Real Estate Advisor, Associate
Broker, Sotheby's International Realty

"For the aspiring business professional, *The Business of Dining* charts a cumulative, career spanning road-map for becoming acquainted with the world of fine dining. Debbie first identifies the questions and customs that enable the young professional to gain comfort and confidence when dining with colleagues and clients. Progressively, *The Business of Dining* provides practical and creative insight (drawn from Debbie's experience on both sides of the table as an advertising executive and restaurant industry insider) into how a maturing professional can thoughtfully impact the group dining setting with seasoned peers. Ultimately, the read culminates in preparing a young professional to draw on their experiences to become an elegant business dining host. Notably, Debbie identifies the perspectives of all constituents in the dining experience (particularly clients and restaurant staff) and how reading and responding to their queues can make for a differentiated evening in both personal and professional settings."

~ Richard Kampert, Vice President - Global Banking
and Markets, Goldman, Sachs & Co.

"A great educational and reference book to teach young sales professionals how to be wonderful restaurant guests and world class hosts for their customers. I certainly wish I had this knowledge and reference as I was beginning my sales career!"

~ Steve Crowe, Fortune 50, Global Sales Executive

"The Business of Dining is a fabulous guide to the full dining experience. I'm planning on keeping a copy on my phone so that I can reference it when ordering wines, hosting events, and the like. I'm sure to return to the handy bullet points, diagrams, and glossaries regularly. I only wish that I had access to something like this sooner—I imagine that I could've dramatically improved many of my previous dining experiences had I not been quite so intimidated by some of the finer points of fine dining. It really makes me appreciate what goes into the meal (and the experience overall)."

~ Justin Hulbert, Director of the Psychology Program
at Bard College

"Where was Debbie von Ahrens and *The Business of Dining* when I was starting out? For years as a financial journalist, I entertained and interviewed sources over steaks, salads and just about everything else mentioned in this book. Bottom line: I would have loved a cheat sheet like this. No matter. Thank goodness von Ahrens has hit the scene now. There's no end to what I learned from this important guide. In our world of social media and online communication, manners and a beautiful in person meal, set correctly, well ordered, relaxing and comfortable couldn't be more important. That's what von Ahrens serves up here. Read this book. Take notes. And enjoy!"

~Walecia Konrad, financial journalist and content producer.

To receive guests is to take charge of their happiness during the entire time they are under your roof.

-Jean Anthelme Brillat-Savarin

DEDICATION

For my beloved daughter, Emily, whose unwavering love and
support have filled my life with immeasurable joy and meaning.
You have touched my heart in unique and profound ways.
Thank you for being an integral part of my life's journey.

TABLE OF CONTENTS

PART 4: MENUS, FOOD, AND WINE

NOTE FROM THE AUTHOR

My journey in restaurants has brought me so much pleasure and so many wonderful memories, from both sides of the table. I hope that after reading this book when you enter a restaurant, instead of just expecting a meal, you will have more of an understanding and appreciation of all that has been done on your behalf by the restauranteur and staff, and by doing so you will realize the stage is set and the cast waiting for you to orchestrate a beautiful evening.

You have the tools—take the time to think of whom you are meeting, where you are going, and what would make it even more special. Create those unique and magical moments and enjoy them.

PREFACE

RESTAURANTS OFTEN SERVE AS A backdrop to the big moments, as well as the small ones—family celebrations, dates, girls' night out, and business deals. And although they are one of my favorite destinations now, it took time for me to understand how to fully utilize them to both orchestrate and enjoy these moments.

In 1978, I moved to New York and transferred to NYU. I was thrilled to be in the city, but I needed a job to pay for school and living expenses. That's how I found myself walking through the gold revolving doors of One Fifth, a chic restaurant in Greenwich Village, owned by George Schwarz. The second I walked through the doors, I was transported into the world of the elite; jazz played in the front room and a long mahogany bar led to the back formal dining room. The staff was dressed in black and white, serving food that appeared delicious and abundant. It was clear that every single thing in the restaurant was chosen to enhance the experience of the patron. I felt like the luckiest girl in New York when they offered me the job.

One Fifth exposed me to a world I had never known and quickly embraced. The expectations for service were high; there were weeks I was studying more for the restaurant than I was for my classes at NYU, and I loved it. And while I learned a lot about food and wine from the menus, my education also came from listening and observing other servers and our guests. This knowledge would come to serve me in every facet of my life.

After I graduated I went to work in advertising sales and marketing. My comfort and knowledge in restaurants put me at ease with the two-martini lunch crowd and with men in their steak houses—not an easy feat for a woman in the early '80s. Entertaining is part of the job and doing it well can set you apart and give you the upper hand.

After twenty-eight years of working my way up the corporate ladder, I retired to spend more time with my family. Several years later, when my daughter went off to college, I wanted to do something but wasn't quite sure what that something was.

After many conversations and much soul-searching, I realized I wanted to go back to the restaurant world. After all, I had never really left it; I had just been sitting on the other side of the table.

My friends and colleagues assumed I wanted to return as a manager, but I didn't. I wanted to be involved with the food, the wines, and the clients. I wanted to be a waiter or server.

I tried to reach out to George, the owner of One Fifth, but sadly he had passed, so I wrote a letter to Keith McNally, one of New York's top restaurateurs. We had worked together at One Fifth. I met with some of his managers at Balthazar, trailed at Minetta Tavern, and then met with Roberta Rossini Delice, his CEO. They hired me to be a server at Augustine, a beautiful French bistro in the Beekman Hotel, with Michelin-star chef Marcus Glocker.

While working at Augustine and later at Balthazar, I loved watching and guiding new executives through their first big business meal or deal, seeing their confidence grow with each step. My goal then was to elevate the dining experience for patrons so they would truly enjoy the efforts of the chef and restaurant. Now I hope that my stories and experience from both sides of the table will aid in your success and equip you for wonderful dining experiences that will build relationships and create lifelong memories.

Part 1

———————

LIFE STORIES AND DINING LESSONS

Chapter 1

USE YOUR STRENGTHS

My first business lunch was at Barbetta, in the theater district. It was stunning and by far the most formal restaurant I had ever been in. As we entered, I noticed our host's cheeks reddened and the client's posture stiffened. It was not what they were expecting.

I think we stayed only because the maître d' seated us so quickly that it was hard to escape. It seemed daunting with silverware endlessly lined up on both sides of the plate. None of us were from that white tablecloth world.

Grateful for my restaurant background, I looked at them and said, "Start at the outside and move toward the center." They looked at me, relieved, then ordered their martinis. After all, it was advertising—in the '80s.

After that, more and more sales managers started inviting me out with clients on a fairly regular basis. It hadn't occurred to me at the time that my ease in restaurants and knowledge of food and wine made me a welcome addition to the table. I was comfortable, therefore making others comfortable. Spending time with the clients and the company's executives, listening to their conversations, and watching how they interacted was such a learning experience. And, the more clients I knew, the more valuable I was to the company.

Here are some other important lessons I've learned.

KNOW WHAT YOU ARE ORDERING

People don't always know what they are ordering, and price might sway them. While I was waitering one night, a young woman ordered soft-shell crabs. Although not cheap, they were the least expensive of all the crab choices.

As I saw her struggling to eat them, I quietly walked over and said, "You eat the whole thing." She was delicately trying to unshell them, as you would do with every other type of crab. She looked up with the most appreciative smile.

Another night a tourist yelled at me for bringing her raw meat. I explained that steak tartare is served raw. Steak tartare tends to be the lowest price steak on the menu, and I am guessing many have ordered it not knowing it is raw meat.

In my first job out of college, a colleague and I would go to a restaurant for lunch every payday. When we decided to have sushi for the first time, we found ourselves in a cool two-story restaurant in Midtown. The combo plate handled the ordering quandary for us, and we navigated the chopsticks taking one item at a time. But just as Mark, my cohort, put a large green piece into his mouth, a waiter came flying from the stairs and others ran to our table as well. The green was wasabi, Japanese horseradish mustard that is very hot and spicy.

It was too late. The entire piece of wasabi was in his mouth. He looked like he was out of a cartoon—bright red cheeks, eyes bulging, I could only imagine the steam coming out of his ears. As he went to grab the water all the waiters stopped his hand as they opened sugar packets for him to eat. The water would have spread the spice, but the sugar stopped it.

We asked a lot more questions about what we were eating after that.

HOMEWORK CAN BE FUN

Brandon, one of my favorite bartenders from Augustine, had worked at a seafood restaurant for many years and could describe every fish and oyster in exquisite detail. I insisted that we go out for oysters one night.

We went to Crave Fishbar on the Upper West Side. They had eight different types of oysters, which we sampled side by side and then discussed them. I wanted to be able to identify the differences between their tastes and textures.

The first thing I realized was that I had never tasted a West Coast oyster before—and they were delicate and delicious. They have deep round bellies and exquisite sharp scalloped edges, unlike the East Coast oysters that are flatter and brinier. As the night progressed it wasn't just Brandon who was sharing his wisdom, but the waiter jumped in with suggestions, as did the bartender. It was a totally fun experience.

So many people love oysters. An enjoyable night out with a client or friend might be going to an oyster bar and sampling several types, or for that person with limited time, you might suggest happy hour for oysters and wine. It is fun, feels decadent, and is very tasty!

THE IMPORTANCE OF LISTENING

One day, I was on a client call with an account executive who introduced me to a top supervisor at one of the largest advertising agencies in New York. The supervisor had a reputation for being very tough. Trembling inside, I smiled, and we had a pleasant conversation. She asked if I had heard of her, and she was surprised that I wasn't intimidated by her. She knew her reputation. Perhaps she was impressed with my brashness or whatever because she asked if I wanted to come to their Christmas party that night.

I wanted to get to know her, so I went. She smiled and I introduced myself to the group. Time passed and the open bar became a cash bar. Her glass was near empty, and I asked if I could buy her a glass of wine. She said she was going to be leaving soon.

I quickly offered, "How about a half glass?"

She smiled.

Before she could leave, I ran to the bar and ordered a glass of wine, asking the bartender to just pour it halfway. She accepted it with a smile. We wound up staying for hours. I learned so much by just listening to her and her colleagues; I had a blast.

A year or two later, I was at a bar known to be a big advertising hangout. It was packed. The bartender served me a half-poured beer and said, "This is from your friend at the end of the bar." I looked and there she was. Our eyes connected, and we nodded and smiled. We ended up having a strong business relationship that lasted for years.

Many years later, when I was waitering and found a patron still eating or enjoying a conversation with no end in sight but had a near-empty wine glass, I would ask if they wanted another. If they hesitated, I would ask if they wanted a half glass. After a moment and a smile, most would say yes, and those that did would usually stay well beyond that half glass.

Chapter 2

BE CREATIVE

WHEN I FIRST STARTED IN sales, I had a very limited expense account. That meant I had to be creative. Some of my most memorable moments came from those frugal and inventive times.

I had a client that was responsible for all the Pepsi business in New York. My competitors were taking him to every hot restaurant and every luxury suite with endless food and drinks to watch the Yankees, Mets, Giants, and Jets games that he wanted to go to. How was I going to compete?

One day, I called to see if he was available for lunch. He was. I asked him to meet me at the corner of Fifty-Second and Sixth Avenue. I made sure I had cash, and once we were together, I asked him what type of food he was in the mood for. He looked at me puzzled. We proceeded to eat food from some of the most incredible food carts in the city. He couldn't believe we were doing this, but the conversation flowed, and it was a fun afternoon.

Several years later when I had VIP tickets to a small gathering with Paul McCartney, he was the first person I called—it's all about balance and creating moments.

MAKE A PLAN

Every year, there was an annual industry holiday party. Media companies bought tables and hosted their largest advertising clients. It was held at the Waldorf Astoria, in the Grand Ballroom, and there was always a name entertainer. Afterward, everyone would go to the Bull & Bear in the lobby of the Waldorf and meet up with tons of advertising executives from all over the country. It was like being invited to the prom— who was going and who would be left in the office? I was on the cusp and wanted to be asked. When I found out I wouldn't be invited, I came up with a plan.

I teamed up with another salesperson and we invited eight of our top clients to our luncheon. We reserved a round table for ten at a restaurant downtown in Chinatown. It was BYOB, so we brought lots of wine. We met the clients in the subway, assuring everyone would arrive together and on time. We put the subway token into the slot for each client and were on our way.

The food was amazing, the wine was endless, and the conversation was hilarious. Our clients were sad when it was time to leave.

I knew we had to leave by a certain time so we would be the first to arrive at the luncheon's after party at the Bull & Bear. Our clients were thrilled as we walked in and secured the best seats at the bar. Within minutes everyone came down from the luncheon and we mingled. It was assumed we had come down with everyone else. It was great, and our relationships were forever sealed.

DO YOUR HOMEWORK

Every business has a few spots they gravitate toward; get to know them and find a few hidden gems that you can introduce people to.

Word of mouth and restaurant reviews are very important, and the internet has endless places to seek out possibilities: Resy, The Infatuation, Instagram, Foursquare, Eater, OpenTable, Tripadvisor, Yelp, Zagat, and many others can help guide you. These websites are incredible in giving you the most up-to-date information on restaurants and clubs—use them.

When selecting a place, think about everyone's preferences, not just yours. You might love steak houses and know all the FOH (front of house) that will make sure you are taken care of, but to others, it might feel stuffy and old guard. A French bistro might be a great alternative.

I had a client that offered limited times for meetings and would not meet outside of the office. When she said she was bringing her daughter to the office for Bring Your Daughter to Work Day, I took that as my opening. I asked if I could take them to high tea that afternoon. After she thought about it for a minute, she accepted the invitation.

We had an incredible afternoon. None of us had ever gone to a high tea before, so we enjoyed the experience together. The tea, tiny sandwiches, and pastries, all displayed so elegantly, were splendid. And I do think she appreciated that her daughter saw that they were being treated as important and special.

I am a firm believer that people notice and appreciate when you put an effort into knowing what they would like, and what might be special for them, which makes the entire experience incredibly gratifying.

FIND YOUR HOME

When I want to establish myself as a regular at a restaurant, I go to the bar a few times to get to know the bartender. Not only do they know the ins and outs, but part of their job is to help make you feel welcome.

Eating at the bar has many incentives. It is a comfortable and friendly space, which can be both intimate and social. It can be a wonderful alternative if you are dining alone but don't want to sit at a table by yourself. It also serves as a great spot for awkward or difficult conversations because you don't need to make direct eye contact for the entire meal.

One time when I was in Seattle waiting for my red-eye flight home after a long week of sales meetings, I went to a lauded restaurant downtown. There was a wait for a table, so I sat at the bar. I was about to order a glass of wine but instead asked to see the wine list. They had Chassagne-Montrachet, which was one of my favorites. Although a bottle just for one seemed a bit too extravagant, it seemed the perfect way to finish the week. The bartender had never had Chassagne-Montrachet and was delighted when I offered him a glass.

He recommended the Dungeness crab, which I had never had before. It was so delicate and delicious. That coupled with the wine and wonderful conversation with the people next to me made for a very memorable night.

Two years later I returned to Seattle. I couldn't remember the name of the restaurant but knew the area. After looking for a bit, I found it. I sat at the bar and was about to order a glass of wine, but instead looked at the wine list. I saw they had Chassagne-Montrachet and ordered it.

The bartender asked if I was in the entertainment industry and lived in New York. After a moment I realized that I had done the same thing two years earlier. So again, I made myself comfortable and enjoyed the wine, food, and conversation. It became my go-to place in Seattle.

Chapter 3

HAVE CONFIDENCE, YOU BELONG

SMITH & WOLLENSKY WAS MY steak house of choice. I was particularly comfortable at the Grill, which is on the side of the building at Forty-Ninth Street and Third Avenue. It offered lighter fare and wasn't as pricey, which seemed less intimidating. The staff welcomed their regulars by name and always managed to find a table, even when they were jam-packed.

After many years of frequenting The Grill, Tommy Hart, the general manager insisted I move to the front room. I was now a vice president at a television station, and he felt I should join the boys in the front dining room. As I resisted, Tommy physically took my briefcase and proceeded to walk me and my client through the kitchen into the front dining room. He introduced us to every staff member along the way.

Tommy gave us a great table in the front and sent over a bottle of wine. I had arrived. I got nods of welcome from the various tables. The NFL guys were there every Friday, and so were many of my top clients.

Whenever I had a client meal, a bottle of wine was usually waiting on the table. Great restaurants treat their regulars like family, and the staff makes sure you look like a superstar in front of your guests.

GET TO KNOW THE STAFF

While I was working at Balthazar, a couple came in three days in a row for a late lunch. They loved the vibe of the restaurant, so they just kept coming back. Their two sons were going to be joining them that weekend and they wanted to take them there for dinner. I was talking to the wife outside as the husband was inside trying to make a reservation with the host. Sadly, the place was fully booked, and the host said we couldn't accommodate them.

I asked them to wait a moment. I went back and talked to the manager, explaining how they had been there the past three days, were incredibly pleasant, and wanted to share the experience with their sons. I asked if there was any way to squeeze them in. The manager checked the reservation list and went to speak with them. They agreed to come in a bit earlier and would be out by a given time when the table was needed for another party; they got the reservation.

When I started my shift that Saturday night, the host gave me a note to stop by table 62, which was in the VIP section. I smiled as I approached and saw it was the couple with their two sons. They just wanted to say thank you. They shared that they were delighted to get the table and informed me that management sent over two glasses of Champagne. It was lovely seeing them, and it made me happy that the manager had made a note to send complimentary Champagne.

IT IS ALL ABOUT YOUR GUESTS

If you are hosting or suggesting a location for a group, it is important to think about the individuals invited as well as the overall group dynamics when selecting the destination.

Once when I was working at the television station, our management team was invited to a launch party for a new division within our corporation. The general manager, two other department heads, and I, all women, were on the invite list. It should be noted that our television station would be the largest client of this new division.

The president of this new division selected the New York Athletic Club for the event. We were shocked but agreed that we would go for twenty minutes and then leave. It was very insulting to us that he chose a club that didn't allow women members. Women weren't even permitted to enter without a male member there to greet them.

Nobody wants to go to a place where they are not welcome. This was a very bad start to this new relationship—it was mentioned often and was never forgotten.

My recommendation is to not support establishments that have excluded any group in the past. You want everyone to feel comfortable and enjoy themselves.

Chapter 4

BE A GREAT LISTENER

WHEN I WAS WORKING AT One Fifth, *Saturday Night Live* would take over the back dining room every several weeks. Gilda Radner, Bill Murray, John Belushi, Jane Curtin, Dan Aykroyd, and others would come with some guest stars and crew.

One night Bill Murray walked up to me and asked for a rum and water. He stepped away, came back, and said "Make it a double rum and water. "

He stepped away for the second time, then said, "Make it the biggest rum and water you've ever made."

I went to the bartender with a carafe and asked him to make the biggest rum and water he ever made.

When I delivered the carafe to Bill Murray, he looked at me curiously. I explained it was the biggest rum and water we ever made.

He grabbed the carafe, then me, and gave me the biggest noogie ever. It was magical.

WAITERS NEED TO LISTEN TOO

Waiters should enhance your experience by making recommendations based on the parameters you have given them. This means price, number of courses, etc.

When dining at a very well-known Italian restaurant in Greenwich Village the waiter thought we made fantastic choices but said we should order more. My daughter and I love to try different things and are usually quite content with sharing two appetizers and an entrée, or maybe three appetizers and a side. We told the waiter we thought we had ordered plenty.

He followed up with, "If you want the full experience."

My daughter gave me a look to hold strong—we had a plan and knew our eating capacity. I told the waiter that I thought we were fine, but he was persistent and made me feel intimidated, as if we would be missing out. I caved and we ordered one more thing.

I was mad at myself the entire dinner for feeling bullied into ordering the additional dish, my daughter was miffed, and we were too full to have the dessert we wanted.

What started as a fun night, turned into a not-so-great night. I sensed the waiter was trying to get our bill up. Ironically it would have been more if we had ordered the dessert and after-dinner drinks we had planned on. The waiter was shortsighted, and the restaurant lost a customer.

It is your night, not the waiter's. If you have a waiter or server who is trying to upsell everything, or only recommending the most expensive items on the menu, don't let them. You can politely point it out to them, so they know it is not okay or appreciated.

SERVERS SERVING THEMSELVES

In 1997, I was planning my wedding for an August afternoon in NYC. I met with the manager of the beautiful restaurant Café des Artistes. I said I was interested in booking the entire restaurant on a Saturday afternoon for a luncheon, but they would have it back by 5:00 p.m. so they could be open for dinner. I reminded her that most restaurants in the city were empty for lunch during August (this was in the '90s), so it should be an easy ask. The restaurant held about sixty people—I guaranteed fifty-four. We discussed a prix fixe menu with three appetizers and three main course options. She asked about the dessert. I said we would come back to that. We agreed on the price, but I never mentioned that it was for my wedding. When she later realized what the luncheon was for, I could tell she was a tad disappointed she hadn't secured a higher rate.

We ordered a wedding cake from them, selected the wines, and requested tap water unless someone specifically wanted sparkling water. Everything was spectacular, but I noticed during the luncheon that there were opened half-filled bottles of sparkling water everywhere. I commented to the waiters. There were only four people I knew who preferred sparkling water. The waiter was trying to pump up the bill, and they did. The bill had over $500 for water for fifty-four people. The manager and I later discussed it and came to terms. Water aside, the staff did a beautiful job, and it was a wonderful event.

When a waiter overpours wine or water, it doesn't go unnoticed. A great evening can be ruined if guests leave seeing wine glasses filled with undrunk wine and multiple bottles opened with a fair amount left in each one. The bill might be larger that night, but the tip percentage will probably be less and there is a good chance that if the customer is feeling like they got ripped off, they probably won't return. And chances are they will mention the negative, first, to their friends, which might overshadow their positive comments. This type of service is shortsighted and should not be condoned or tolerated.

CHALLENGING CUSTOMERS

Although the waiter has to deal with difficult customers, that behavior can impact other tables as well as the vibe of the very table that difficult customer is sitting at.

Once a woman said, "I want a dirty martini."

I asked if she wanted vodka or gin.

She asked for the complete list of vodkas we served; I recited all seven. She paused and looked at her friend who had already ordered a dirty martini.

She said, "I want it like hers."

She didn't know her vodka preference and wasn't listening when the others ordered.

I said, "She ordered a Grey Goose dirty martini up."

She paused and said, "Yes. That's what I want. Except I want it really dirty. How much olive juice do they use?"

I hadn't a clue. I suggested that I order a very dirty martini and she could always add more olive juice.

"No" she insisted, "I want it really, really dirty."

I smiled and nodded, then walked away. I ordered her a Grey Goose dirty, dirty martini up and brought extra olive juice on the side. When I checked on the table, I asked her how the martini was. She said good, but it could use a bit more olive juice. I pointed to the small carafe of olive juice I had placed in front of her when I brought the martini.

"Oh, yes," she said. But she never added it.

"What oysters do you have? I like the little ones."

I listed the six varieties we were serving that night and let her know that our smallest were all from the West Coast.

"I only want oysters from the East Coast, but I want the smallest ones."

I repeated that our smallest oysters were all from the West Coast, but I could order her the smallest from the East Coast if that is what she preferred.

"No! I want the smallest, period," she demanded.

I suggested that she get four Wellfleet from the East Coast and try two Kusshi from the West Coast, which was the absolute smallest we were serving. Only after her friend insisted she try them did she agree.

Her friend, the other woman at the table, tried to help as the two men ignored everything while they enjoyed their one-to-one conversation. Her husband looked at me during one of her question sessions with a half smirk, like she's your problem now. He was right, but I knew that after two hours I was done with her, and he wasn't. I gave him a smug smile back.

As they were leaving, I asked her what she thought of the oysters.

"Oh, I loved those little Kusshi ones."

She never acknowledged the suggestion.

As a customer, you get to give reviews, which is empowering. But you should be aware that now many of the restaurant apps also allow servers and staff to add comments to a guest's profile that can be seen only by the restaurant, so they can develop a profile of their customers. Ninety-nine percent of the staff comments are about the wine ordered, favorite dishes, allergies, anniversaries, and things that will help make the next dining experience even more memorable. But there is also room for comments about problematic and difficult customers. Be gracious when you are out and respectful of the staff, don't be the 1 percent.

Chapter 5

ESTABLISH YOURSELF AS THE HOST

HOLIDAY BUSINESS MEALS CAN BE stressful, so it's incredibly important for the host to set the tone and parameters so that everyone can relax and enjoy the event.

This is a story of a lunch that almost went awry while I was a waiter at Augustine. It was a party of ten and I wasn't sure who the host was. I looked at the group and asked if anyone wanted a glass of wine or something to drink.

A young woman said loud and proud, "I just want water."

Everyone looked from side to side, not sure what to do—it was water for everyone. This was not going to be a fun lunch. I briefly discussed the menu and after a few minutes went to take the order. The young woman who ordered the water quickly said that she was ready and wanted a salad. I asked if she wanted to start with anything.

She said, "No, just a salad and water—that is all I want."

The next person sheepishly ordered a sandwich. A reminder: we were in a stunning restaurant with an amazing menu and a Michelin-star chef, and it was a holiday luncheon.

I finally realized who the host was and asked if she wanted to start with anything.

She looked at me and asked, "Have the others ordered anything to start with?"

"No, they have not," I offered, then added, "Would you like me to suggest a few things that they might enjoy sharing?"

"Yes," she replied.

"Would you like a glass of wine with your lunch?"

She smiled and said, "Yes."

I then asked, "Would you like a glass, or should I get a bottle for the table?"

She smiled again, looked at her guests, and said, "I'm having wine—would anyone like to join me?"

And that did it. She was now in charge of a relaxed, fun, holiday luncheon. By her taking charge and giving some direction, everyone now knew they were there to enjoy themselves and have a pleasurable time.

The luncheon was a success. Everyone loved trying the various appetizers, sipping wine, getting to know each other, and enjoying the various conversations. By the time the dessert menu came, they all seemed comfortable ordering something. The host seemed to be very appreciative, and I am confident she will take the lead the next time she takes a group out.

CREATE A MOMENT

Once at a steak house, I overheard a client say that she would love a steak, but it was just too big, and she wasn't that hungry. I asked if she wanted to share one.

We each ordered an appetizer and split the steak; it was the perfect amount. We were both happy with the choice.

Whenever we dined together after that she would look at me and ask if we were doing "our thing." It had been a great bonding moment and intimated we had a long history together. Making a moment a memory is special and should be appreciated.

PRESENTATION MAKES A DIFFERENCE

Many restaurants use their house wine glasses for bottles of wine up to a certain price point, usually about $120, then more refined stemware for bottles priced above that.

If you are dining at a time when not all the restaurant resources are in demand, you might request the Burgundy glass for your eighty-dollar bottle of Pinot Noir. If the glassware is available, they should oblige.

Changing or upgrading the glassware gives the appearance of a more expensive, special bottle of wine. A more elegant, refined glass will be appreciated by your guests, and everything just tastes better in a nicer glass.

From the server's perspective, I liked using some of the better stemware at the beginning of the evening even if the wine wasn't in the higher price range. It was appreciated by the diners, helped set a tone in my section, and was a wonderful cue for the other diners to take a serious look at the wine list.

At One Fifth, they have beautiful antique decanters that decorate the shelves. I once saw a manager use one of them to serve negronis. I asked if we were allowed to do that for other tables, and she was like, "Of course, it's all about the guest experience."

I was telling one of the regulars about the decanter, and they said they were coming in with a large group the following week and could they use them? We had the decanters chilled and waiting. We brought iced glasses with orange twists to those that wanted a negroni—everyone did once they eyed the beautiful decanters. We poured the drinks, then left the decanters on the table for them to refill their glasses at their leisure. It was a standout night and made the experience both special and memorable for everyone.

Two families were dining together, with a total of three kids, ages four to six years old. The parents were having cocktails and one of the children wanted a glass of milk. I filled the glass halfway up and told the mother I would bring the other half when needed. I thought it best to pour a bit at a time to help avoid spills.

When it was time to bring more milk, I poured it into a small six-ounce carafe, which looked very cute. As I approached the table, the kids were all staring at the carafe wide-eyed and smiling. I proceeded to pour the milk into the glass.

The other kids insisted, "I want milk! I want milk!"

Their mother shared a look with me, then with them. They

quickly promised they would drink it all, and they did. Presentation matters.

NAME CARDS

A guest came in early one night regarding a reservation and asked to see which table they would be seated at. He spoke with our host for a few minutes, then left. He returned about twenty minutes later with beautifully handwritten name cards that he strategically placed on the table. He knew exactly where he wanted everyone to sit and wasn't taking any chances.

The name cards elevated their evening, and the small detail did not go unnoticed by Anna Wintour, Vogue's editor in chief, and those who were seated next to her.

Attention to detail and extra effort are usually appreciated and will help to ensure you achieve your goals.

Chapter 6

WINE NOTES

AT THE ORIGINAL ONE FIFTH, in the '70s, the wine captain would present the bottle of wine to the person who ordered it, then open it standing to their right (beverages are presented and served from the right, food from the left).

If a sommelier (suh-muhl-yay), also referred to as a "somm," presents the bottle, they usually present the bottle to the host, then take it to the wine table to open and taste, then bring it back to the table and present again to the host to taste.

As I was observing this recently, I gave it a bit more thought and realized that taking the bottles to the wine table for the sommelier to taste allowed them the opportunity to try twenty or so different wines on a given night. It also made it easy for them to have a wonderful discussion about that specific wine with the guest. What an incredible way to offer sommeliers the opportunity to broaden their knowledge and expertise while on the job and make for a more informed dining experience with the guests.

LEARN FROM THE BEST—THEN SHARE

I was hosting a birthday dinner for a friend who loves cheese. So, I decided that we should start the evening with a cheese and wine pairing. Since I am not well versed in cheese, I looked up some suggestions online. After a bit of research, I had a list of cheeses and grape varieties that would pair well with them.

I took my list and headed to 67 Wine. Although they are always a great source of wonderful wines, I think the conversation was heightened because I showed them the types of cheese I wanted to pair the wines with. We agreed on four specific wines, and I headed to Murray's Cheese on Bleecker Street in Greenwich Village with the wine list.

At the counter, I said that I was putting together a cheese and wine tasting and needed assistance. Natasha came forward and said, "I am sure I can help you out. May I see which wines you selected?"

She talked me through the various kinds of cheese and offered samples as she shared her thoughts on why they would pair beautifully with the wines.

As we were finishing, she said, "You have to try Rogue River Blue—it was named World's Best Cheese at the 2019 World Cheese Awards in Bergamo, Italy, the first time a cheese from the United States won the award."

The cheese was incredible. I bought an additional piece so the guest of honor could take it home.

Murray's Cheese includes the name and description of each cheese on the packaging. I used that information to create a menu complete with the details about the wine I was pairing them with. This allowed us to have an informed conversation about them and also helped us remember what we enjoyed and wanted to buy in the future. The night was magical.

When you have the opportunity to go to a great cheese shop or wine store, I suggest going inside and asking questions. People that are good at what they do enjoy sharing their expertise—let them! And enjoy the benefits.

COURSING THE MEAL

Smith & Wollensky has always been a Midtown favorite and the background for so many of my business deals throughout the years. They always make you feel welcome and help to create special moments and memories.

They have been hosting Wine Week for over thirty-five years

and I recently went with two friends. Although we were excited, we knew we couldn't possibly eat the three to four courses needed to pair with the ten wines they were pouring. We also knew we were committed to tasting all ten wines and weren't in a hurry.

We were seated and read the menu.

- They poured a Prosecco and Pinot Grigio.
  We perused the menu as we enjoyed the wine.
- They poured a Chardonnay and rosé.
  We shared six oysters.
- They poured a Pinot Noir and Sangiovese.
  We shared the Wollensky steak salad.
- They poured a Côtes du Rhône, Shiraz, and Cabernet Sauvignon.
  We shared 2 orders of lemon pepper chicken and one creamed spinach.
- They poured Quality Bordeaux from a jeroboam.

We had ordered one appetizer, three mains, and a side dish for the three of us, but by coursing the meal this way, (three courses instead of two) the food was paired beautifully with the wines, and the time was spaced out. It felt much more elegant, festive, and pleasant.

As to the Wollensky style, they poured the ten wines as advertised, but they made it memorable when they brought out the final wine in a jeroboam and presented it to the room.

A jeroboam is the equivalent of two magnums or four bottles of wine. I had seen a jeroboam in a restaurant as part of the decor once or twice, but this was the first time I had seen one opened and poured, and I was a recipient. Everyone in the room smiled acknowledging this special moment.

IT'S ALL IN THE DETAIL

We had made reservations at Balthazar to celebrate a friend's birthday. Before we even walked in, we were going to start with their seafood tower and something sparkling to drink. We were ready to celebrate.

To our surprise, upon entering, the host welcomed us to Balthazar's Twenty-Fifth Anniversary and thanked us for joining them. We were seated at a great table and immediately greeted by the waiter presenting a bottle of Taittinger Champagne, compliments of Balthazar. Every table was given a bottle to celebrate their anniversary.

They then presented each of us with a beautiful keychain with a Balthazar *B est. 1997* engraved as a memento. This was far above and beyond any expectation.

We continued our dinner by pairing beautiful wines with fabulous foods starting with lightest to heaviest, finishing with their infamous steak au poivre, duck shepherd's pie, onion tarte, frites, and a magnum of Gigondas.

As we were leaving and wanted to give a special thank-you to the host and managers, they then presented us with the *Balthazar Cookbook*, signed by Keith McNally. It was an incredible night to remember. There was no way you could leave without acknowledging how much thought and preparation they had put into this evening and celebration. It was an incredible acknowledgment and thank-you to their clients and an illustration of the generosity, love, and spirit that restauranteurs share through their establishment. Spend time finding restaurants that bring you joy and go back again and again.

Chapter 7

JUDGMENT DAY

WORKING AS A WAITER IN a restaurant after thirty-seven years had its challenges. My memories were of the great nights, chic clientele, amazing food, and wine. That was true for my most recent dining experiences as well, except I was the one sitting at the table asking the questions, not the one responsible for knowing the endless ingredients, wines, pairings, allergies, etc. So, there was a vulnerability to being the one wearing the apron and asking the person dining what they wanted to eat and drink.

When working downtown near City Hall I was miles away from my Upper West Side neighborhood. I suspected I would eventually run into people I knew, but I felt safely tucked away downtown. After several months I did spot one of my old media buyers/ clients at a table. I walked over to the banquette and said "Pam, move over!" as I scooted into the banquette.

She screamed, "Debbie! Oh my God, what are you doing here?"

"Working," I said.

"No, really?"

I got up and showed her my outfit, complete with an apron. "I always loved restaurants, so here I am."

"Oh my God, that's great!" she exclaimed, as we continued to catch up.

A few weeks later I asked a customer if he had worked in the advertising business, as he looked familiar. He said he had been but was retired and visiting the city with his family. I told him my full name.

"I know you. You didn't hire me!"

"I didn't hire a lot of people," I responded. We then talked about people we knew and how the business had changed. It was fun catching up.

On another night, Patrick, one of my favorite waiter/managers from Smith & Wollensky was dining with his wife, whom I had known from the advertising world. He had waited on me for over twenty years and now the tables were turned. I realized that I was excited at the prospect of reciprocating the generosity and hospitality he had shown me.

There is something so satisfying to me when you are entertaining someone that notices and appreciates all the details; it becomes an elevated experience because it is shared. It was fabulous seeing Patrick and his wife again, reminiscing over the past and enjoying the present.

And then, one day an owner of a company that I had worked very closely with at WNYW/FOX5 came in. I took a breath, knowing she would be surprised to see me as a waitress, and said, "Hello, Rachelle."

She looked at me with a bewildered, blank stare. I was totally out of context for her. I wasn't wearing a business suit, wasn't carrying a briefcase, didn't have an appointment, and was wearing an apron.

I put out my hand, smiled, and said "Debbie von Ahrens."

She took my hand and in disbelief said, "Debbie von Ahrens, from Channel 5, with the beautiful daughter?"

"Yes," I said,

"What are you doing here?" She couldn't put it all together.

"Having fun," I said. "Let me take you to your table."

She introduced me as I pulled out the chair for her.

She quietly said, "This is Debbie von Ahrens. She once had a very important job at Channel 5."

My heart sank and I held back tears.

I looked at her friends and said, "I like to think that I am still important," as I smiled and turned away.

It doesn't matter which side of the table we are on; we are all important and should appreciate those we encounter and respect the work we have all done to get there.

Part 2

TABLE SETTINGS, SILVERWARE, AND WINE GLASSES

Chapter 8

TABLE SETTINGS

Salad fork, dinner fork, plate, knife, soup spoon

THE PLACE SETTING SETS THE tone of the meal. It might be informal or very formal. There might be several utensils lined up on each side, or just a few. But as long as you are familiar with their place you will be able to imagine the courses and navigate the meal effortlessly.

Many restaurants start with a simple place setting that includes a salad fork to the farthest left, then a dinner fork, the plate in the center with the dinner knife to the right with the sharper edge facing inward. This picture has a simple setting with a soup spoon added to the right of the knife, so you can assume a soup will be served first, followed by a salad, or appetizer since the salad fork is also there.

The place setting will be adjusted once the order has been

taken. The server should clear and reset each course. However, if you go to a restaurant with a prefixed menu or the table is already set with a lot of silverware and glasses, and you are not sure which to use, just start at the outside and continue inward.

Top: Bread plate, butter knife, teaspoon, dessert fork, water glass, red wine glass, white wine glass
Bottom: salad fork, dinner fork, salad fork, plate, dinner knife, escargot fork

This second illustration is a bit more formal and takes us through dessert. The bread dish and butter knife are placed on the left and/or above the forks. Glasses are to the right. The water glass is above the knife, then to the right, and slightly below that is the wine glass. If a red and white wine glass are set, the red wine glass would be between the water glass and the white wine glass because the white wine (lighter) would be poured first. When it comes to using glasses, like silverware, start with the farthest out and move inward. The silverware placed above the plate, a fork, and a spoon, is for the dessert.

Once the silverware is used, it should be rested on the plate, not on the tablecloth. If the course is finished and the waiter is taking your silverware, it will be replaced with fresh silverware shortly.

In the above illustration you could assume that bread and butter will be served, the first course is probably escargot, followed by an appetizer, then entrée, salad, and dessert. There will also be white wine, red wine, and water served.

Chapter 9

USING THE SILVERWARE

American Style

THERE ARE TWO STYLES OF using your utensils while eating—American and Continental. In the American style, the fork switches hands in a zigzag fashion. The knife is initially held in the right hand, the fork in the left, but the knife is put down (resting on the plate) after cutting just a few bites of food and the fork is switched to the right hand to pick up the cut food to place in your mouth. The fork is again switched to the left hand when the knife is picked up by the right hand to cut a few more bites, and the switching continues. Never grip your silverware or hold it as a "fist"—it is distracting and looks crude. When in doubt think of holding a pencil for the fork.

Continental Style

In the European or Continental style, you hold the fork with the tines facing down in the left hand and the knife in the right. When a bite-size piece of food has been cut, you spear it with the fork and continue with the left hand to your mouth. The knife stays in the right hand and is used to guide food to be eaten onto the back of the fork in the left hand. Both utensils are held with the handle along the palm, extending out to be held by the thumb and forefinger.

In either case, when resting during the meal, your utensils should be placed in a V shape, or the knife could go on the rim of the plate. When finished with the meal the utensils should be side by side at the center of the plate pointing from twelve o'clock to six o'clock, or four o'clock. Americans usually have the fork tines faceup; Europeans usually have the fork tines facedown. In today's world, the angle is not as important, just that they are together, side by side, signaling that you are finished with your meal. The fork and knife should not be in an X position because it could make it difficult for the server to clear.

SILVERWARE
FORKS

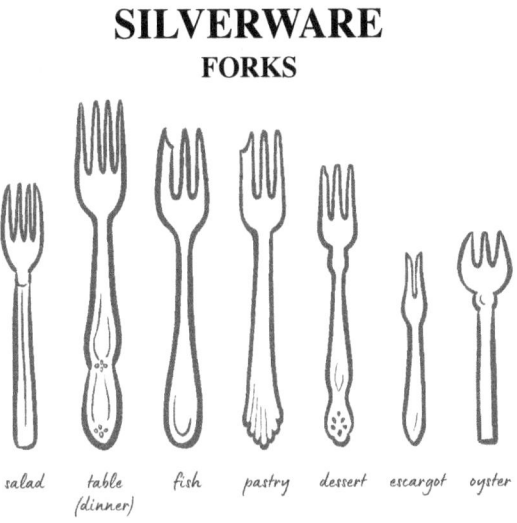

salad   table   fish   pastry   dessert   escargot   oyster
(dinner)

Salad fork—is a short, broad four-tine fork. Used for salads and other appetizers or starters. If the salad fork is closer to the plate with the dinner fork to its left, assume salad will be served after the entrée.

Table/dinner fork—the largest or longest fork with long tapered tines made to spear the food.

Fish fork—the left tine is slightly larger than the others or might have a notch on the side, this is to help remove the bones and skin of the fish. Fish forks were originally made of sterling silver so they wouldn't react to the citrus used on fish.

Pastry fork—is a specialized fork six to seven inches in length, a little narrower than a salad fork. The left tine of a pastry fork is extra wide with a flat edge to aid in cutting firm desserts, such as fruit pies or tarts.

Dessert fork— is a little narrower than a salad fork with three or four plain tines.

Escargot/snail fork—is a small, slender, two-prong fork used for snails (escargot) that are served in the shell.

Oyster/cocktail/seafood fork—a small narrow fork with curved tines, usually three or four. Used for shellfish, oysters, and sometimes for certain small plates.

KNIVES

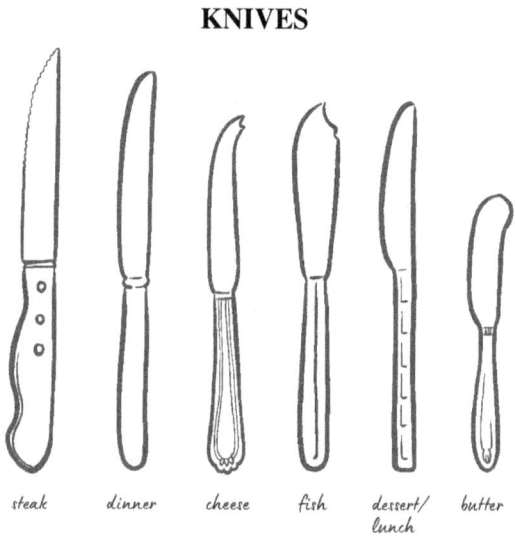

steak   dinner   cheese   fish   dessert/   butter
                                         lunch

Steak knife—a sharp table knife that often has a serrated blade and a wooden handle. In addition to steaks, I like to use a serrated knife for dishes with pastry dough, using a light sawing-type motion so it doesn't crush the pastry crust.

Dinner/table knife—the largest of the knives with a blade sharp enough to handle just about anything but steak. This knife is always to the immediate right of the plate with the sharper edge facing inward.

Cheese knife—a long narrow blade with a curved, fork-tipped end so you can cut the cheese with the blade and spear it with the tip.

Fish knife—a thing of beauty. It has a scalloped-shaped blade with the end being just pointed enough to help pick small bones. The flat blade is useful in separating the skin from the fish.

Dessert/luncheon knife—about eight inches long with a narrow blade and rounded or pointed tip.

Butter knife—short, with a dull and rounded edge, or pointy tip, used to spread butter and jams.

SPOONS

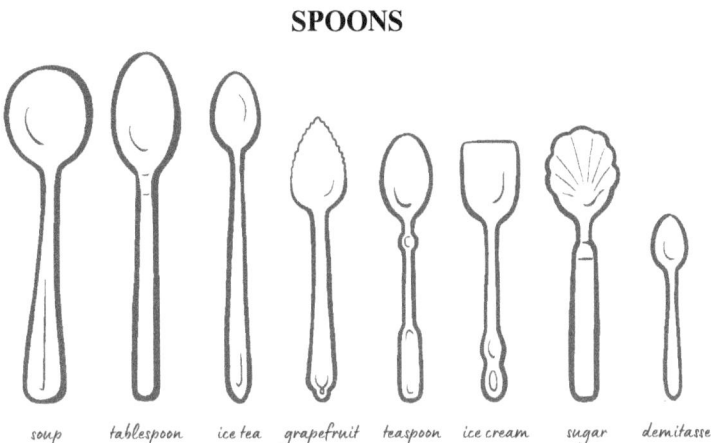

soup   tablespoon   ice tea   grapefruit   teaspoon   ice cream   sugar   demitasse

Soup spoon—its length is the same as a tablespoon, or a tad shorter, with a rounder and deeper bowl at the top.

Tablespoon—quite large and elongated. It is generally around eight to nine inches, similar to the dinner knife, which is usually nine inches.

Iced tea—long and slender handle traditionally served with drinks in tall glasses.

Grapefruit spoon—same size as a teaspoon, sometimes narrower, with a tapered top with serrated teeth.

Teaspoon—small spoon used for coffee, tea, and soft foods.

Gelato/ice cream spoon—the size of a teaspoon or smaller with a flat edge like a shovel.

Sugar spoon—used for serving granulated sugar. A deeper, rounder bowl than a teaspoon, usually with a beautiful scallop design, like a seashell.

Demitasse spoon—is smaller than a teaspoon and is traditionally used for espresso.

Chapter 10

WINE GLASSES

Pinot Noir Bordeaux Burgundy White Champagne Sherry

WINE GLASSES ARE SHAPED TO capture and enhance the bouquet, maintain the temperature, and help keep the effervescence lasting longer in Champagne and sparkling wines. Hold them by the stem to help protect the temperature.

Red wine glasses are usually larger and have a wider bowl than white wine glasses. Bordeaux glasses have a smaller bowl than Burgundy glasses. The bigger bowl offers a larger surface for air, allowing the oxygen to break down the tannin in the wine, making it softer on the palate. We taste with our mouths and our nose, so the larger space allows us to enjoy the bouquet.

Although not always the case, some say if you are not sure which glass to use, look at the shape of the bottle. Generally, a Bordeaux wine comes in a taller square-shouldered bottle, and a Pinot

Noir or Burgundy comes in a larger bottom-based bottle and sloped shoulders. The square-shouldered would go in the Bordeaux glass, and the large bottom bottle in the Burgundy glass.

In addition to the smaller bowl, white wine glasses are less curved, more tapered, and still offer enough space to enjoy the bouquet.

Champagne was once served in a coupe, a wide-mouth short stemmed glass. They are fun to look at but are not ideal because the short distance and large surface made the bubbles disappear almost immediately. Next was the flute, but this too has its drawbacks, too narrow to smell and you almost need to toss your head back to drink it.

Those who order Champagne or sparkling wines on occasion seem to love the look and feel of the flute, which has an essence of elegance and celebration. Many that enjoy Champagne more regularly seem to prefer an elegant white wine glass. It is a bit broader but still protects the bubbles and gives you enough room to enjoy the bouquet and texture.

Pinot Noir glass—tall like Bordeaux glasses, but with a larger bowl offering a wider surface for the wine to breathe, tapering in to capture the aroma, then slightly flaring out.

Bordeaux glass—usually a tall wine glass with a smaller bowl than a Burgundy glass.

Burgundy glass—has the largest bowl, offering the widest surface for the wine to breathe. The top tapers in to help capture the aroma.

White wine glass—has a smaller bowl than Bordeaux glasses and is tapered at the top to capture the aroma. Its size and shape help maintain its temperature.

Champagne flute—a stemmed glass with a tall and narrow upright bowl. The shape helps to maintain its temperature and effervesce.

Four-ounce ice wine or sherry glass—like a small or mini white wine glass with a small bowl that tapers in to hold and enhance the aroma.

Part 3

THE DINING PROCESS

Chapter 11

SELECTING THE DESTINATION

WHETHER IT IS FOR BUSINESS or pleasure, selecting the destination is the first step. When you walk into Balthazar there is a vibe, a look, an electricity that permeates the room. Seafood towers, steaks, martinis, and Champagne fill the tables. Less than a mile away, Frenchette offers a different experience. The aesthetics remind me of the Four Seasons—quiet, elegant, and chic. The cuisine might be similar, and both offer an incredible backdrop for business and pleasure, but the experience would be very different at each venue.

There is a restaurant for everyone and every occasion. It is important to take the time to think of what the goal of the evening is and to select a destination that will help you achieve that goal. No time that you spend researching restaurants and their menus is wasted.

RESERVATIONS

Making the reservation is the next step. If you want dinner to be on the quiet side, it is best to go early. The room begins to fill by seven or seven-thirty, leading to prime time including noise and activity.

It is important to share all the relevant and important information when you make the reservation. For example, if you are celebrating a birthday and would like a candle in the dessert, request it then. Additionally, it is smart to alert them of any allergies at that time.

If you want to bring your own bottle of wine or dessert, ask ahead, don't just show up with it and expect them to accommodate you. Some restaurants will not permit anything from the outside, others will have a plate charge or corkage fee.

A plate charge is generally a per-person fee for everyone at the table. The corkage fee is charged per bottle. If a restaurant serves wine but is allowing you to bring in your own, you might ask if there is a restriction on how many bottles, as they might allow only one or two. Corkage fees may be hefty to discourage bringing in outside wines (fifty dollars per bottle). These fees make sense because you are taking away the ability for the establishment to sell you similar items, so the fees may reflect the profit they might have made had you purchased it from them. They are also servicing your items with glasses, plates, and utensils.

ARRIVE ON TIME

As a guest, you should arrive on time or a few minutes early. If very early, wait at the bar and take care of your check before you join the group.

As a host, you should arrive several minutes early. Although all your requests should already be in the computer system, it is smart to make sure the restaurant's staff is aware of allergies and important details. This will also establish you as the host, which the waiter always wants to know. By being there early you can see where they are seating you and if there are any issues you can take care of them before your guests arrive. If you want to preorder a bottle of wine or make sure you get the bill, this is the time to request it.

CHECK YOUR COAT

When most people walk into a fine dining establishment, there is no question that they will be handing over their coat and any briefcase, tote, backpack or bag to the coat check person. It is understood that you are there for the food and ambiance and it is not acceptable to ruin the look of the restaurant with clutter, coats or bags hanging messily from the chairs. It is also assured you will tip that person generously as you exit.

So, why, when given the choice, do so many keep all their possessions when going to a very nice restaurant that might not have a Michelin star? Don't they realize that the restaurateur is equally as concerned with the look of their restaurant, the comfort of all guests, and accessibility to the table?

When I was working as a server, post-pandemic, a table of five brought their coats, computers, backpacks, and shopping bags to the table. These things took away from the elegance of the restaurant, were messy, spilled into the next table's space, made it awkward for every person walking past the table as the puffer jacket added a solid eighteen inches to the circumference, and made it difficult for the waiter to get close to the table. They appeared to be oblivious to their mess, the inconvenience it caused others, and even to themselves when trying to exit the table for the restrooms.

Remember that this is not your home, where I am sure your guests' coats are comfortably hung in the hallway closet. If there is a coat check, check your coat, unless you are at a casual place with hooks nearby.

And remember, it is a service job—coat check employees take care of and protect your items. This is surely worth a two dollar or so tip (per coat).

Chapter 12

THIS WAY, PLEASE

TABLES ARE ASSIGNED BY THE host or manager before that shift begins. They will usually go through the list of all the reservations for the evening, and make sure that the best tables are available throughout the night for their top clients.

Many restaurants do indeed have an A, AA, or VIP list. Resy and some other online reservation apps can note how many times you have frequented the restaurant by reservations you have made on their app and offer notes on those making the reservation. Requests are usually written next to the guest's name so the manager can review them with the waitstaff that will be serving them.

Once you are all seated, the waiter will welcome you and help orchestrate the night. This usually begins with a cocktail, mocktail, or wine. They will want to get that order immediately, so you can enjoy your drink while you consider the menu.

If you order wine by the glass, it is fine to ask the waiter if you may taste it first. Unless you are familiar with both the vineyard and the grape, it may be very different than what you were expecting. If new to wines, I recommend requesting to taste two wines (available by the glass) unless you are confident in your selection. It is nice to compare wines side by side, and two options allow you to learn more about what grapes you like or prefer.

Once settled, the waiter should go through the menu and highlight the evening's specials. This is a great time to ask for recommendations. Restaurants spend an incredible amount of time and money to make sure that their front-of-house staff is well versed in the food and wines that are being served. They review menus and ingredients nightly. Many have tastings so the staff can better explain the dishes versus just reciting the ingredients. Some restaurants offer their staff wine training and cocktail classes or tastings, so waiters and managers can offer suggestions that pair your food with wines for a better dining experience. None of this is easy. It takes a lot of time and effort to learn, memorize, and expedite. Good waiters don't just take orders, they are there to elevate your experience.

While discussing the menu and specials, servers will want to know about allergies or food preferences. If they don't bring it up, those with allergies must. In many restaurants, the waiter is responsible for sharing allergy information with management and the chef. The waiter should also let you know what is being ordered at the table that the person with the allergy should stay away from.

The chef always wants the full order up front. They are executing multiple courses for many tables at a time, so seeing the entire order helps them put the pieces of the puzzle together and orchestrate it beautifully. This also helps the waiter to know how to set up your table for the evening, which plates, utensils, and glasses will be needed, when to bring wine, etc.

A waiter helps to keep your evening moving forward, guests served, and the table cleaned and clear. They should be attentive but not overbearing and keep the host informed if things are taking longer than expected. They should also make sure wines and beverages are served at the host's pace. Waiters are there to help make your meal a memorable one, so it is smart to engage with them for a more enjoyable experience.

MAKING THE MOST OF YOUR DINING EXPERIENCE

- Be prompt, polite, and engaged.
- If you are running late, text the host or call the restaurant.
- If it is a party of more than four people and you are early, wait at the bar until the host arrives. They might have a plan for where

they want you to sit.

- If you order a drink at the bar before the group is there, pay that bill before you join them.

- Reading through the menu ahead of time (online) gives you the ability to carry on a conversation while merely glancing at the menu when at the table.

- On a diet? Keep it to yourself, no need to discuss it with the group.

- No snapping fingers at any of the staff.

- Some waiters will introduce themselves; some prefer to remain nameless. If you insist on asking their name, it is polite to say yours as well. Even if a name is shared, it is best not to overuse it for it can be construed as condescending.

- Talking while the server is going through the specials means they probably have to repeat everything. Be polite and pay attention, there will be plenty of time to talk afterward.

- Listen to what your host orders or suggests and try to stay within that price range.

- When ordering, many still consider it to be polite for the women to order first, usually from oldest to youngest.

- The waiter wants to get as much information from you as possible when taking the order, so stay engaged with them until they move on to the next person. Ordering a burger doesn't tell them everything they need to know. How do you want it cooked? Do you want it with cheese or french fries? Would you like ketchup, mustard or mayonnaise? Did you want to start with something?

- If you really want to order a salad but are afraid it might be awkward to eat, ask if they can chop it in the kitchen.

- If wine is ordered but you don't want any, tell the waiter as they are putting the wine glasses down, or if the glass is already on the table, simply hold two fingers over the glass as the waiter approaches you and say, "No thank you."

- Wait until everyone is served before you begin eating, an exception would be if the host insists that you begin while the food is still hot.

- Salt and pepper get passed as a pair.

- If something is being passed to someone else, and you want it, too, wait until after they get it, even if it is passing right by you.
- Pass dishes to the right and offer to hold the dish while the person to your right serves themselves.
- If you drop silverware on the floor, just leave it, unless there is a server close by that you can hand it off to. You don't want to bring dirty silverware to the table.
- Used silverware should not touch the table, it should be rested on the side of your plate.
- Keep pace with the group. Try not to be the slowest eater or the fastest. Best to finish within minutes of the host. If finishing early, leave the last bite and finish with the group.
- Dirty dishes will be cleared once everyone has finished eating. It isn't polite to shove the dishes away from you, or your chair away from the table while the dishes are still in front of you.
- If you have to go to the bathroom, be observant as to what is happening. If the waiter just reset the table, it is a signal that your next course is on the way. Wait if you can or try to hurry.
- If you find that you usually need a light to read a menu I suggest buying a penlight. It is used by nurses to look at a patient's eyes, so they are very easy on the eyes, don't disrupt other diners, are the size of a pen, under ten dollars, and very effective.
- Know when to leave.

NAPKINS

Napkins should be placed on your lap; folded in half with the fold near your torso. When using the napkin, try to use the inside area near the fold so the stains or marks stay inside and away from your clothes. If leaving the table, you should fold the napkin and place it to the left of your place setting or on your chair seat, pushing the chair in. If wearing lipstick, it is best to blot your lips, not wipe, before drinking any beverage. When finished, fold the napkin, and put it to the left of the plate.

PHONES

This one is hard to put into practice, but phones don't have a place at the table and should be put away. However, if you are expecting an important call, let your host know that you are sorry, but there is a call that you need to be available for. Keep your phone silenced and facedown. When the phone call does come, excuse yourself from the dining area and handle it as quickly as possible.

If you want to take a picture of the food, make sure the host is fine with you doing so. The flash should be off, so you don't impact other diners. Take the picture quickly and put the phone away, the same for a selfie.

Chapter 13

CONVERSATION, WAITERS, AND GOOD GUESTS

WHETHER AT A BUSINESS FUNCTION OR out with friends, friendly, lively conversation is key to a good time. Stay away from one-word questions and answers. Good conversationalists usually keep current with books, theater, film, and current events, and most stay away from politics, controversial topics, and questionable humor.

Body language plays a part in the conversation. Good posture, arms in an open position versus crossed, relaxed not stiff, eye contact, and a smile are all very welcoming to others. The key is being comfortable and open, and offering that to the group.

- When seated at a table next to people you don't know, always introduce yourself.
- One common question is "What do you do?" Try not to give just your title or company, turn it into a conversation, something engaging, but not a long monologue.
- Talk to people sitting next to you as well as across from you—try not to leave anyone out.
- Be a great listener, everyone loves a good audience. If new to the group, a good way to learn more about the people is to let them speak and listen to what they are saying.
- Don't interrupt and pick safe topics—nothing too personal. Books, theater, museums, TV shows, films, music, and food are welcoming topics.

- Eye contact with those you are dining with as well as the staff is important. It makes everyone feel comfortable and part of the experience.
- Don't feel pressured to drink alcohol, but if you do, here are a few tricks if out with a heavy drinking group: ask for a "light drink" meaning light on alcohol. If ordering a mixed drink like gin and tonic, ask for a tall glass, there is generally more tonic or soda in that. You may also request extra tonic on the side and continue to add to the mixed drink.
- Be mindful of good behavior—politeness is always appreciated.

THINGS YOUR WAITER WANTS YOU TO KNOW

- The waiter can control only so many things. If you are annoyed with the table you are being seated at, say it before you sit. It is disruptive to everyone if you change tables after the water has been poured. If they can't change your table, don't let it ruin the night.
- Having a waiter stand there while you are carrying on a conversation is outwardly rude. A waiter is there to try to make everyone comfortable and move the meal forward at an enjoyable pace. Acknowledge the waiter and try to get your cocktail order in at a relatively quick speed. You will have plenty of time to talk afterward.
- Order what is on the menu. Menus change, so spending five minutes describing a dish that you once had at the restaurant is not going to bring it back.
- When the waiter puts your order into the computer, allergies and special requests such as dressing on the side are input into the computer as well. The food order is put in order of where each person is seated. So, moving where you sit after the order has been taken is annoying to the waitstaff, and makes the service look sloppy.
- Your waiter is your waiter, going around them can create annoyance or miscommunication.
- Waiters and busboys need access to the table. They need to place things on it as well as clear things from it, so sit relatively close to the table, not with your chair pushed far away, making it near impossible for them to manage the table. Also help the waiter along the way, especially if your table is in an awkward or hard-to-reach

location.

- Beverages are served from the right with the right hand. Food is served from the left and the left hand; the plate should be positioned with the protein closest to the diner.

- If it is awkward to pour from the right because of how the table or chair is situated, then serve open-armed, or in front of the patron with the left hand, almost like a hug.

- In most cases, waiters and busboys are trained to clear the table only when everyone has finished eating each course. All clearing should be done from the right side, with the right hand.

- Kids are your responsibility. Don't assume that the restaurant offers crayons or special kids' cups unless you are in a real family-style restaurant that caters to kids. You should have enough things to engage your children while out. If they are messy, clean up after them. If you want them to eat immediately, just let the waiter know.

- Many restaurants plan their reservations based on ninety minutes for a two-top and two hours for a four-top. Higher-end fine dining, Michelin-star restaurants plan for much longer time than that.

THINGS TO CONSIDER AS A GUEST

When at a business meal, or meeting new people, it will take some pressure off if you order things that are simple to eat. Something you eat with a fork and knife, no heavy sauces that might spill or stain, nothing too slurpy, messy or difficult to eat. Remember the goal is the people; the food is secondary.

You should also be cognizant of the price. One shouldn't necessarily order all the most expensive things on the menu or all the lowest-priced items—both will be noticed.

It is important to look to the host as a guide when ordering. We will look at this more in the next chapter. The waiter is also there to assist you. A waiter should understand your comfort zone and try to recommend within that zone making your night the priority, not theirs.

Chapter 14

HOSTING THE MEAL

WE'VE GONE THROUGH THE STEPS or process at a restaurant, now let's look at it from the host's perspective so we see how it all comes together for a memorable evening out.

Before arriving at the restaurant, I highly recommend that you look at the menu online. Being familiar allows you to be in the moment, conversing with your guests. It is particularly great looking at the wine list online since they seem to be in a small script that can be difficult to read in a dimly lit restaurant. It also gives you time to research their wines a bit more, helping you to find something special in your price range. I suggest having wine options, then ask your waiter or somm if there is anything in that category or price range that you might have missed.

When hosting the meal, it is best to be the first there, so you can see where the table is. If you are unhappy with its location, it is much easier to try to change tables before everyone arrives. Know where you want to be seated and where you want others to sit. A guest of honor should be seated to your right. The best seat usually has the best view. Being a thoughtful host means that you will take charge in a very understated way, never bringing attention to yourself, simply helping move the evening forward seamlessly and pleasantly. A thoughtful host should make sure that people are seated so the conversation will flow, and everyone will be and feel included.

Arriving at peak hours can feel fun and lively, but it is also the hardest time on the servers. The waiter can welcome only so many people at one time and the bartenders can make only so many drinks in the limited space they have to work in. So, you will probably get a nice welcome and have to wait just a few minutes. But the staff is prepared for this because it happens every night. Maybe make a 7:00 reservation instead of 7:30 or if you like the later side, tables start opening again right around 9:00 or 9:30 p.m. in NYC.

The first question from a waiter is generally about which water you would like—tap, flat or sparkling. If flat or sparkling are presented in a closed bottle for your approval, there is usually a fee, and some prefer to pour their own, so it is not wasted. Bottles that you are paying for should never be brought to the table without your permission. If some people are drinking flat or tap and some sparkling, you might ask the waiter to bring a different glass for the sparkling, so no one is confused when refilling.

As host, you will be setting the tone as soon as you begin greeting your guests. As you are seated, everyone will welcome cues from you—"I have been looking forward to a martini all day." "May I see the wine list?" "What kind of oysters do you have today?" "Are there any specials this evening?" You are giving a ton of information by asking these questions. Guests would know that you are going to order a cocktail, so they can, too. Wine will probably be ordered for the table, and all should be prepared to order more than one course. They know what is expected and you have put them at ease so they can relax, converse, and enjoy.

The waiter will want to get the cocktail and wine order as soon as possible. By ordering the wine early you are allowing the waiter time to get it, open it, make sure it meets with your approval, and have it ready for when your food arrives. In most restaurants, someone else must get the bottle of wine for the waiter. If the restaurant is busy, it could take time. This way the waiter will not stress about having the wine ready for you when you want it. It gives you the time and space to be with your guests, uninterrupted by questions.

Note: If you arrived during prime time and the waiter alerts you that the bar is very backed up, meaning a twenty-minute wait for a cocktail, you might want to order wine or something the waiter can get without waiting in line for the bartender.

ORDERING YOUR MEAL

As host, you will lead the night, so offering simple suggestions for your guests will be appreciated. While looking through the menu, you might suggest an appetizer or two, which will let them know that they should be prepared to order more than just an entrée. Or if you hear some "aren't very hungry" comments, you might suggest ordering a few appetizers for all to share. You are trying to create a moment, a memorable time for everyone, not just a meal. It doesn't take much effort to make it special. Simply show your guests that you were looking forward to this evening, their happiness is important to you, and you want to make sure they have a great experience.

Sharing can be a great way to try different dishes, but it is important to let the waiter know exactly what your expectations are, so they can prep the table, making for a smoother dining experience. Do you just want the dishes placed in front of you and you will share or alternate, or do you want family-style with the dishes in the middle of the table with serving spoons and share plates?

Appetizers and desserts are simple to share; entrées can be more challenging. If just two of you are sharing an entrée, you may ask if they can split the dish in the kitchen. There might be a small charge for doing so, but it is usually worth it. If sharing a burger, you might ask them to cut it in the kitchen. It will not be as messy and will be easier to share at the table. If sharing a large rib eye or steak with several, you might ask if they would slice it in the kitchen, making it much easier to share and pass at the table. When sharing with a group, use the serving utensils, take an appropriate amount, make sure there is enough for everyone, and pass it to the right.

If you are budget conscious, you might say, "I heard their burgers are great." This flags that you are not going to order a big entrée. If you prefer that not everyone orders an appetizer, you may say, "I was going to order the goat cheese tart and pâté to share for the table. How does that sound?" This lets your guests know that you are going to start with shared appetizers.

Ordering everything at one time should result in a better dining experience because it lets everyone know what your overall plan is. The waiter wants to get as much information from "the table" as possible. The more they know what your desires are, the easier it is to make them happen. The more the chef knows, the better they can execute what all the diners want by having what they need at hand. Most kitchens, especially in New York, are incredibly small and have additional work or prep space in a different area or on a different floor. Knowing what they need allows them to orchestrate and time your meal.

The waiter will have an idea if the kitchen is running fast or slow, and what the reservations look like. If there are a lot of large parties that are just about to order, they might try to get you to order before the large parties do, not wanting you to wait too long for your dinner. Or, if a lot of orders just went in so the entrées are going to take a bit longer than usual, the waiter might suggest that you "course" differently. Start with appetizers, then maybe a shared salad, followed by the main course. It is everyone's goal to make sure your experience is excellent, not too rushed, and not too long of a wait.

Some people seem to think that if they give the entire order at one time, they will be rushed. Just communicate that you do not want to be rushed, and a good server will make sure that you are not.

Once everyone has ordered, it is nice to ask the waiter if they think you are missing anything. The waiter should summarize what was ordered so you can then add some nice details. They might realize that a lot of people ordered steaks that are served only with starch; by ordering a few vegetable sides, the meal would be complete for everyone. There is a reason the sides are on the menu; they are the finishing touches.

Once the order is in, you should be able to just enjoy the rest of the night. Stay in touch with the waiter to ensure things continue to move forward.

MOVING THE MEAL FORWARD

When the entrées are finished and the table cleared, you can either offer, "I hope you saved room for dessert. They are known for their crème brûlée." Or, if someone is ordering a tart you can jump in by asking, "Are you having a port with that?" Just enough of a suggestion that dessert and an after-dinner drink may be ordered, or if the night has gone longer than expected, and you are hoping to skip dessert you might say, "This has been great! The night went so quickly," or something like that should flag that the meal has come to an end.

KNOW WHEN TO LEAVE

I think it is fair to be out of a restaurant ninety minutes to two hours after the kitchen is closed or the last table is seated. So, if the restaurant serves from 5:00 to 10:00 p.m., the last tables should be out 11:30 p.m. to midnight.

When you see that there are only one or two other tables left, it is time to finish up, pay, and move on. If you are not ready for the night to end, ask if you can move to their bar or if the waiter could recommend another place nearby that is still open.

It is not just your waiter waiting to go home—there is usually a full team waiting for the last table to leave so they can then do their side work, close out their checks, and clock out.

Transportation late at night can be difficult to get, not necessarily safe, and expensive, so it is good to be empathetic to all.

Chapter 15

ORDERING THE WINE

MANY FINE RESTAURANTS HAVE A sommelier or wine steward, one who is trained in wines and available to discuss the wine list. The more details you give them, the better they should be able to help you select wine close to your description. Do you want white or red? Light or full-bodied? Dry or a bit on the sweet side? A particular country or region? Do you have a price point? They might ask what dishes you will be ordering so they can better suggest a wine that will complement the food.

Five five-ounce glasses are usually served from one bottle of wine. Quick math will show you if ordering wine by the glass makes sense, or if you are better off ordering by the bottle. There is usually a cost-benefit to ordering by the bottle. Knowing that five glasses are generally served from one bottle should also help you to figure out how many bottles you will need for your party. If you have six people in your party, the waiter or sommelier should know to pour a lighter or smaller pour so everyone gets a glass. You can then decide to order another bottle once poured or later. If there are seven or more people and they are all drinking wine, chances are you will need two bottles.

When ordering wine by the bottle, you don't have the luxury of tasting it to see if you like it, you are tasting it purely to make sure it hasn't turned or is corked. So, if you are not sure of the grape or region of wine you want to order, you might let the waiter know you are not sure but are thinking of either a Pinot Noir or a Bordeaux and would like to taste the house wines by the glass from that region to get a better idea. After tasting the two, you will know which you prefer. If you love the one that you tasted, ask if they sell it by the bottle, if not, ask if there is something on the wine list that is similar and in your price range.

The house wines by the glass are generally the lowest-priced bottles in their category. A good restaurant is not going to have a bad bottle on its list. So, if you are looking for the best bottle of lower-priced wines, look to the house wines. The price is generally four times the glass price, plus a few dollars. And since they are offered by the glass, you can taste them before you commit to buying the bottle.

WINE SERVICE

The server will present the bottle of wine to the person who ordered it. The label should be facing up and easy to read. It is important to read the label to make sure it is what was ordered, including the year or vintage. Once accepted, the server will cut and remove foil from the lip of the bottle and the cork, cap if a twist-off, and wipe the bottle lip before pouring. A small tasting pour will then be presented to that person. If the cork is presented, you may look at it and feel it. A cork should not be wet or too dry or brittle. The goal is that the cork kept all the air out of the bottle and all the wine inside the bottle. Next, smell the wine, and swirl to release more of the aroma. You can tell by the smell if it is corked or has turned.

For Champagne or sparkling wines, they will take the foil off, and put their thumb on the cork while undoing the wire cage that holds the cork in place. One should never take their thumb off the cork, always putting pressure on it to hold it in place. The bottle is held at a forty-five-degree angle while the bottle is slowly twisted (not the cork). The cork should ease slowly and let out a small hiss as the air releases, not a pop. Champagne and sparkling wine bottles should never be aimed at a person, and once the cage has been removed a hand or thumb should always be on it protecting the cork from being released.

If you ordered a red wine and a white wine, the waiter should open the white first, then the red. It is recommended to try the lighter wine first, then go to the heavier. Or you might ask one of the guests to try one, while you try the other.

If you know your group, and that they like wine, a thoughtful way to start the night is to preorder a sparkling or white wine, to begin with so it is ready to open when you get there. You are not telling your guests they must drink it; you are simply showing it is going to be a relaxed enjoyable evening, you have thought of them and planned. This takes the pressure off some making decisions about what to drink and allows toasting while cocktails might be on their way.

When tasting the wine, pick up the glass by the stem, look at the wine's color, then smell it to bring in the bouquet and aroma. The smell is an important part of the overall taste—if a wine is corked, you can usually tell by the smell, even before you taste it. If corked, you may notice a browning in the color and the smell will be off. But assuming the smell is pleasant you now swirl the wine. This releases all the aromas that can be detected subtly by the nose. The air or oxygen helps to lessen the mask of alcohol. You can also see the "legs" or lines that come down the glass after swirling. Thinner, lighter wines don't necessarily have legs but more robust wines will.

If a wine is "off" or corked, it will smell a bit moldy, like a musty basement. A heavy raisin smell is another signal the wine might have turned, making a red wine taste sweet. If you do think it smells corked, alert the waiter that you think it is corked, and ask if they would mind trying it first. The waiter will either taste it or call a manager to take over. I suggest this because management usually gets involved when a wine is rejected, so they must taste it anyway. Why take the chance of having the awful, corked taste in your mouth?

If it is corked, the restaurant will know and ask if you want to try another of the same wine, or a different wine. Your palate will be fresh to taste the next bottle. And if they don't think it is corked, then try it, knowing it should be fine. Nothing has been lost. There is usually one bottle every so many cases that may be corked, so it is something to smell and look for. Corked bottles should be identified right away, then the restaurant will be able to return them to the distributor.

Once ready to pour, although it might seem dated, it is still considered appropriate by many to pour wine for the women first, then the men, and lastly the host. The wine glass should never be more than halfway filled. Keep this in mind if you decide to pour the wine yourself, or if the waiter is not there to do so. Most will pour the wine to the largest width of the bowl or glass, so the wine is at the largest possible surface area to breathe. The only time a glass of wine might be more than half-filled is when ordering wine by the glass, some pour three-fourths of the way, depending on the glass size.

READING THE WINE LABEL

Country of origin—this is usually at the top or the bottom of the label. The more specific usually means the more select the wine.

Name/producer—the winery.

Grape variety—the primary grape used. By knowing the grape, you should have an idea of the tasting notes. Not all wines show this on the front label, so look on the back as well.

Vintage—percent of grapes used must be from that year.

Alcohol content—fuller wines usually have a higher alcohol level.

Sulfites—this is usually listed in case of an allergy.

QUICK NOTES ON WINE

- When ordering wine for the table remember that there are usually five glasses per bottle. So, if there are six or more people you might order two bottles.
- Pair like wines with like foods: earthy foods with wines with savory depth like Pinot Noir from Burgundy or Nebbiolo from Italy; think mushrooms and truffles. Sauvignon Blanc and Fume Blanc have a bright, citrus acidity that acts as a fresh squeeze of lemon. They go beautifully with fish, tangy foods with tart dressings, and

sauces.

- Texture or tannins in bold, rich, full-bodied wines can overwhelm a delicate dish. Full-bodied wines go well with heavier, more complex foods. Milder foods are better paired with medium to light-body wines.
- A fun white wine at lunch might be a light refreshing Chablis or Riesling. A nice red would be Pinot Noir something light and easy that won't overpower the food.
- In general, white wines will go beautifully with fish, except a big, bold, buttery California Chardonnay may overpower it. If you want red wine with fish, maybe try Pinot Noir, Chianti or Beaujolais.
- Champagne and good sparkling wines are dry but have just a bit of sweetness that complements salty dishes: oysters, shellfish, charcuterie, as well as most entrées.
- Dry rosé has the acidity of a great white and the fruit notes of a red, which holds up to rich cheese dishes but are also lovely with shellfish.
- Chardonnays from California are silky and full-bodied. Try them with fatty fish like salmon, any fish with a rich sauce, and white meats.
- Steaks go with a wine with firm tannins and structure like California Cabernet Sauvignon; a French Bordeaux; Grenache/Syrah blend from Rhône; or Barolo or Barbaresco from Italy. If you want a white wine with a steak, try Champagne or a California Chardonnay.

The drinking age is twenty-one in the United States. Even if you are having a family function and are fine with your twenty-year-old having a glass of wine, they should not be served, even by you. It is against the law, and you are jeopardizing the restaurant's liquor license by doing so.

Chapter 16

PAYING THE BILL

IF YOU ARE IN A group and splitting the bill, it is best not to exceed three or four credit cards. It might seem like it is simple, but it isn't. It is time-consuming, which takes the waiter away from their other tables, and it is stressful. The waiter is responsible for the bill, so they must get a copy of all credit card receipts, with signatures, and need to make sure the math is correct and complete. Servers are usually told to pick up the signed receipt(s) before the guest leaves the table or restaurant in case there are any issues. If the guest leaves with the signed receipt by mistake, the house or restaurant can still collect their part, but chances are the waiter will not get their tip.

If you joined late, or are leaving early and want a separate check, ask your waiter when you are first seated. They might be able to handle it easily if they know beforehand. When splitting the bill or estimating your portion, remember to add the tax and tip. When splitting the bill assume a 20 percent tip unless the service was below par.

If you are picking up the check, it is nice to arrive early and let the restaurant's host or waiter know. If possible, give the waiter your credit card at that time so there is no argument later. It is always nice to handle the bill away from the table—just give the waiter the credit card before the meal and instruct them to meet you away from the table afterward.

TIPPING/GRATUITY

The new standard for tipping seems to be 20 percent or more for good service at fine restaurants in major cities. If your waitstaff went above and beyond, you might add a small or nominal cash tip on top of the 20 percent. Average service is 15-16 percent, poor service is generally 10 percent.

Most fine restaurants have elaborate computer systems that account for everything, including cash tips. Waiters are responsible for claiming all tips. Most waiters must pay certain percentages of their tips to other staff such as bartenders, food runners, and busboys, so all cash tips must be recognized and accounted for each shift. Many of the top restaurants also work under a "pooled house" system, where the waiters share their tips, not keeping 100 percent of their tips to themselves. Customers might think they are doing the waiter a favor by tipping in cash, but they are not. The exception would be if you tipped on the credit card 15-20 percent and left an additional cash tip. In some restaurants, the waiter would share the 15-20 percent on the credit card and keep the additional cash.

A NOTE ON TIPPING

Some restaurants offer happy hour where select items are 40-50 percent cheaper during a specific time. You might give a larger percent tip at this time because your bill is deeply discounted. Or if eating at a busy restaurant where the average bill is eighty dollars a person and you are only having a bowl of soup and water while you read a book for ninety minutes, it might be best to consider the experience, and tip accordingly.

Part 4

———————

MENUS, FOOD, AND WINE

Chapter 17

MENUS

THIS SECTION BEGINS WITH THE layout of the various menus, how they flow, and what is usually included in them. I will then delve deeper into each category with pronunciation, descriptions, and important details.

COCKTAIL MENU

A designated cocktail menu is usually categorized by specialty cocktails, spirits, wines by the glass, beer, and mocktails (non-alcoholic) if offered.

If you have a favorite cocktail that isn't on the menu, ask for it. Bartenders are well equipped these days to make just about anything, as long as they have the ingredients. Mocktails usually include fresh mint or a fun herb, therefore usually priced somewhere between soda and a cocktail.

WINE LIST

Most wine lists are divided by white, red, rosé, and Champagne. The wines are then separated by region. Some restaurants take it further and list the wines from lightest to fullest within each region. You might ask the waiter if the list is done that way, as it could help you with your selection. More and more organic wines are being added to menus from all over the world. They may have an earthier taste, so it's good to ask for advice.

Many fine restaurants have French and California wines, sprinkled with others from around the world. Many Italian restaurants prefer to offer only Italian wines and Spanish restaurants might prefer to offer Spanish wines, etc.

The wine menu is often available online, and if it is, I think it is smart to look through it ahead of time and find a bottle or two that you like at your price point. When at the restaurant you might tell them what you are thinking and ask if there is anything on the list in that category (meaning price range) that you might have missed.

LUNCH AND DINNER MENU

The food menu is categorized by courses and then usually from lightest to heaviest. I have listed the raw bar even though it is available in very few restaurants.

Raw bar: oysters, clams, ceviche, shrimp, crabmeat, Alaskan king crab, mussels, and lobster. Many restaurants that have a raw bar generally offer a seafood tower or fruits de mer, which includes a bit of everything.

Appetizers: salads and small plates, the first course. If interested in a cheese plate but don't see it on the menu, ask. Some restaurants only list cheese on the dessert menu but are happy to serve it anytime.

Entrées: fish, being the lightest, is usually listed first and dishes continue with the heaviest, usually meat dishes being last. The entrée description should be fairly in-depth, or at least list the key ingredients, and preparation—grilled, roasted, sauteed, etc.

Sides: potatoes and vegetables presented as side dishes tend to be the last thing on the menu and are usually great for sharing and adding special touches.

DESSERT MENU

Most fine restaurants have gifted pastry chefs who create signature desserts along with many popular desserts. The cheese plate may be listed with the desserts along with coffee and tea options. Some restaurants include ports, Sauternes, Amaris, and cordials on this menu as well.

Chapter 18

ALLERGIES

It is important, to be honest about how severe an allergy is because for some it can be a life-or-death situation. If it is just a preference, say that. It is best to note this at the beginning of the meal so the waiter can advise you what might be on the table that you should stay away from. They will then communicate with management and the chef who will work together to make sure you are safe.

You should not assume that you know all the ingredients in every dish, which is why you should repeat your allergy to your waiter when ordering. Some kitchens use peanut oil for the deep fryer, meaning french fries should not be ordered if you have a peanut allergy. Many kitchens use the deep fryer for multiple dishes creating cross contamination, usually with gluten. A small garnish can be fried, carrying both peanut and gluten, but a waiter will know to write down your allergy and add no garnish. Garlic is used in many sauces and sometimes in the water that shellfish are boiled in. I've served steak tartare made with fish oil and desserts made with almond flour. It is always best to ask.

Below are the general ingredients of the different allergies. If you have something that isn't listed, tell the waiter, and be exact.

Allium: chives, garlic, leeks, onion, scallions, and shallots.

Dairy: products made from the milk of other mammals, such as cows, goats, and sheep.

Eggs: fresh as well as dried or powdered egg products, eggnog, mayonnaise, and meringue.

Fish: seafood, but it might be in sauces (Worcestershire), salad dressing, and gelatin.

Gluten: the general name for proteins found in wheat (durum, einkorn, emmer, farina, farro, graham, Kamut, Khorasan wheat, semolina, wheat berries) barley, rye, and triticale.

Peanuts: besides the actual nut, they might be hidden in cookies, baked goods, candy, ice cream, sauces, and the deep fryer if peanut oil is used.

Shellfish: crustaceans and mollusks, such as clams, crab, crawfish, krill, lobster, mussels, oysters, prawns, scallops, seppia, shrimp, snails, squid, and others.

Tree nut allergy: almond, Brazil nuts, cashew, hazelnut, pistachio, and walnuts.

Chapter 19

FOOD DESCRIPTIONS

The following is a list of food available in many of the top restaurants with the pronunciation, short description, and/or a suggestion as to how to eat them. This should help make you feel comfortable with most menus and in most dining situations.

Artichokes—(aar·tuh·chowks) are a thistle eaten as a vegetable. They are usually steamed or stuffed with bread crumbs and fine herbs. When served whole, remove one leaf at a time, and dip the soft end into the sauce. Turn the leaf so the soft side is facing downward toward your bottom teeth, place it just up to where the soft part is into your mouth, and then pull it through your teeth. Put that leaf on the side of the plate.

When most of the leaves are removed you will see the heart of the artichoke or the choke that forms a firm center of what is referred to as the meat. Use a knife to gently scrape or cut the fuzzy part off, then cut the meat into bite-size pieces with your fork and knife. Dip in the sauce (melted butter, olive oil, vinaigrette, hollandaise.) Use the salad fork and knife.

Avocado—(aa·vuh·kaa·dow) has a pit and therefore is a fruit, not a vegetable. They are known to be filled with nutrients and good fats. They may be served cut in half with the pit removed and a dollop of dressing or a filling placed in the center, or it might be simply sliced. Avocado toast has also become a breakfast favorite—avocado smeared on toast, sometimes topped with fried eggs. If the avocado is served by itself in the skin or shell, use a spoon to scoop it out. If served without the skin, use a fork.

Bone marrow—(bown meh row) is usually from a cow. The large bones (usually shin bones) are cut in half, and the marrow is seasoned and then broiled. You might be given a demitasse spoon to lift or scoop out the marrow. It is usually served with toast points as an accompaniment and a small salad, as a palate cleanser.

Bottarga—(bow tar ga) salted, cured fish roe pouch, typically from red or gray mullet, or bluefin tuna. It offers a light briny sea salt taste and is usually served finely grated over pasta.

Bouillabaisse—(boo·yuh·bays) is Provençal fish soup with fish, mussels, and clams, made with tomato, fennel, saffron, garlic, and Pernod. Served with a fork, knife, oyster fork, soup spoon, and discard bowl for the shells.

Bread—when you take a piece of bread or roll from the bread basket, place it on your bread-and-butter plate. Know it is not proper to bite into the whole piece of bread or roll or to butter the whole piece at one time. If the butter or condiment is in a shared dish, do not dip food directly into the dish. Serve yourself, using a spoon or knife, and place some of the butter or topping on your bread-and-butter plate or the main plate. You should tear just a small piece of bread, prepare it, and eat it. Repeat when ready for the next bite. If dipping in olive oil, put some oil on your bread plate and dip. If dipping in a shared bowl or dish is the only option, break off a small piece of bread and dip but never double-dip.

Calamari—(kaa·laa·maa·ree) is Italian for squid, usually grilled, sauteed, or deep-fried. It is not the same as octopus. Use the salad fork if an appetizer, dinner fork and knife if an entrée.

Carpaccio—(kaar·paa·chee·ow) is very thinly sliced meat, served with a generous sprinkling of parmesan or truffles, and drizzled with a mayonnaise-based dressing or served with olive oil and capers. Use your salad fork and knife. Many restaurants offer seafood or vegetable carpaccio as well.

Caviar—(ka·vee·aar) is a delicacy usually served in a small glass bowl sitting on crushed ice. Toast points or blini (small thin mini pancakes) are presented on the side with condiments that may include chopped red onion, capers, grated hard-boiled egg, crème fraîche or sour cream. Caviar is expensive, so if you are adding your own to the toast or blini, take just a small amount at a time. Don't be like Tom Hanks in *You've Got Mail*.

- **Beluga**—(bi·loo·guh) is the most expensive and largest (the size of a pea) with a faint ocean taste.
- **Ossetra**—(o·set·tra) is known for its nutty taste.
- **Sevruga**—(sev·roo·guh) has the strongest taste.

Ideally, caviar should be scooped with a spoon made of mother-of-pearl, bone, or wood. A metal spoon can give the caviar a harsh metallic taste. Use your fingers with toast points and a fork and knife with blinis, unless the blini is small or bite-size.

Ceviche—(suh·vee·shay) is a combination of raw fish, shrimp, lobster, and calamari with onion, cilantro, peppers, and tomatoes that are cured or cooked by adding citrus—lemon or lime juice to marinate. Salad fork and knife if needed.

Charcuterie—(shaar·koo·tr·ee) is a selection of cured meats such as salami, ham, speck (Italian cured, smoked meat), saucisson (French salami flavored with garlic and black pepper), and a terrine or pâté. Served with toast points, crackers or bread. Served with a salad fork and knife.

Chicken paillard—(pai·ar) is a chicken breast pounded paper thin, usually grilled, topped with arugula, tomatoes, balsamic, and olive oil. Served with a steak knife.

Cioppino—(chuh·pee·noh) an Italian American fish stew originated in San Francisco. Depending on the exact ingredients it might be served with a soup spoon, oyster fork, fork, knife, and a discard bowl for the shells.

Clams—(klams) can be served raw, steamed, grilled, deep-fried, baked or in pasta. For raw clams, put the sauce on top of the clam and then tilt it into your mouth, eating in one bite. For steamed, hold the open shell in one hand and remove the meat with the other using an oyster fork. Dip in melted butter or broth and eat in one bite. Place the empty shell on the rim of the plate, or in a discard bowl. Littlenecks from Long Island and cherrystones are both very popular. Deep-fried clams are prepared out of the shell so just use a fork and knife. If the clams are served in the shell in pasta, free a few of the clams from the shell with your fork, put the shells on the side of your plate or in a discard bowl, and toss and twirl pasta with clams to eat.

Cornichon pickles—(kor-nuh-shaan) are small, tart, crunchy pickles. A good garnish for pâté or steak tartare.

Crab

- **Alaskan king crab legs**—giant crabs from the Gulf of Alaska. Just the legs and claws are served. The delicately sweet bright white meat has a red outer edge. Served warm with lemon and drawn butter, or chilled with lemon and dipping sauces.

  Start by cracking the shell with a nutcracker and take the meat out with an oyster fork, while shells go in a discard bowl. Finger bowls are usually brought to the table after eating crab legs.

  Finger bowls are simple bowls with cool to warm water, a lemon slice, and a napkin on the side. Just lightly swirl your hands one at a time and dry. Some restaurants might bring warm towelettes with lemon instead.

- **Dungeness crab**—a two-to-four-pound crab from the West Coast. The crab meat is succulent, sweet, moist, and tender with salty hints. Served warm with lemon and drawn butter, or chilled with lemon and dipping sauces.

  To eat, remove the shell, clean out the organs, break away the legs from the body, then break the body in half. There are little cavities of meat in the body, so use the oyster fork to get the crabmeat. Break open the legs and claws with the crab cracker, then use the oyster fork to get the meat. Served with crab crackers, oyster fork, and a discard bowl.

- **Soft-shell crab**—three and a half to five and a half inches, green–blueish crabs that turn red when cooked. The crab is caught at the beginning of the molting season, so it is a seasonal dish. Soft-shell crabs are usually sauteed or fried, which gives them a light crunch with buttery soft sweet meat inside. You eat the entire crab with a fork and knife.

• **Stone crabs**—known for their large pinchers on the front of their body with brownish-red claws with black tips. The claws have a very hard, thick shell protecting their delicate meat, which is firm, succulent, and sweet.

The claws are cracked with a mallet. Hit the claw several times, turn, and hit again. Remove the meat and dip it in the sauce holding it by the pincer. Mustard sauces are frequently recommended. Use a mallet and oyster fork.

Crudités—(kroo·di·tā) raw vegetables served on a platter with various dips.

Crudo—(kroo·dow) is raw fish topped with a drizzle of fresh citruses such as lemon juice or vinegar and olive oil. A garnish of lemon zest, red pepper, caper berries, grapefruit or mint to finish. Served with a salad fork and knife.

Cuttlefish—(kuh·tuhl·fish) is a marine mollusk, known as seppia, of the squid or octopus family.

Dim Sum—(dim soom or dim sim) Chinese meal of various dumplings and small dishes.

Entrée—(aan·tray) is the main course in the U.S. but can be a small course in other countries.

Escargot—(eh·skaar·gow) are snails usually served in garlic butter with bread on the side for dipping. If the escargot is presented to you in a shell, there will be a small escargot fork, usually two-pronged, placed to the right of your knife and a pair of tongs to help hold the shell. Hold the tongs in your left hand and use the fork in your right hand to get the snail out of the shell. Toothpicks are quite helpful in getting snails out as well. Don't be shy about dipping your bread directly into the garlic butter. Ask for more bread if needed.

Fines herbs—(fin erb) chopped herbs–parsley, chervil, tarragon, and chives. Wonderful with soups, sauces, vegetables, and egg dishes.

Fish filet—(fuh·lay) is the cut of fish. The flesh of the fish is cut to exclude the bone. Although boneless you should always be careful when eating because fine tiny bones may still be present.

Fish steak—fish that is cut crosswise, so you have the flesh of the fish on both sides with the bones in the middle. The most popular is probably salmon steak.

French onion soup—usually topped with melted cheese over a large bread crouton. The soup is under the cheesy barrier. Take a small amount of cheese that you twirl on your spoon, exposing some of the bread. Then take the swirled cheese to the side of the bowl and cut it into smaller bites, using your spoon against the rim of the bowl. You could use your knife if the spoon is not working. Served with a soup spoon, fork, and knife.

Fruits de mer—(fruit tee mah·reh) is a tower of shellfish both raw and cooked served on shaved ice with a layer of seaweed. The tower usually includes oysters, clams, mussels, shrimp cocktail, ceviche, and lobster or crab. Served with mignonette sauce, cocktail sauce, pink mayonnaise, and lemon. You should be given a nutcracker, an oyster fork, and a discard bowl for the shells. The waiter should bring a finger bowl or hand wipes with lemon when you finish eating to clean your hands.

Gremolata—(greh·mow·laa·tuh) green sauce made of chopped parsley, lemon zest, and garlic.

Guanciale—(gwaan·chaa·lay) pork cheek or jowl of the pig.

Hamachi—(huh·maa·chee) sushi-grade buri or yellowtail.

Haricot vert—(heh·ruh·kow vurt) are long, slender French green string beans.

Herbs de Provence—(erb pruh·vaans) mix of dried thyme, rosemary, fennel seed, lavender, marjoram, bay leaf, basil, and sage. Great with grilled foods.

Hors d'oeuvre—(or derv) are small bites, usually passed or on a buffet.

Hummus—(hum·us) is a spread or dip made from chickpeas, tahini, olive oil, lemon, and spices.

Lobster—(lob·stir) served chilled, grilled or steamed. The legs and claws have a lot of meat and are incredibly sweet. Start by cracking the leg or claw with a nutcracker and take the meat out with an oyster fork. Pull the small legs and suck the meat out. Separate the body from the tail, then cut the tail in half, on the softer bottom side. The tail meat should come out easily—dip it in melted butter and enjoy.

If served chilled it will be served with lemon and cocktail or other dipping sauce. Served with an oyster fork, fork, knife, nutcrackers, and a discard bowl.

Mushrooms:

- **Chanterelle mushrooms** (shan·tr·el) are the most popular wild mushrooms, trumpet-shaped, meaty, earthy, and fruity with a delicate flavor. Great in soufflés, sauces, pasta, soups, and egg dishes.
- **Morel mushrooms** (mr·el) are considered a delicacy. Their cap has a honeycomb appearance. Savory, great with meat, poultry, pasta, and soups. Used in French cuisine.
- **Porcini mushrooms** (por·chee·nee) are similar to portobello mushrooms. They are meaty and nutty, with a smooth creamy texture. Used in Italian cuisine.
- **Portobello mushrooms** (por·tuh·beh·low) are field mushrooms that are dense with a rich taste. Portobellos have a very large flat cap that makes them perfect for grilling and roasting. They are great in sauces and pasta and can almost substitute steak when grilled.
- **Shiitake mushrooms** (shuh·taa·kee) are grown mainly in Japan, China, and Korea. They have a light woodsy flavor and aroma. They are savory and meaty and go great with meats and sauces.

Mussels—(muh·slz) are usually served in a pot with a white wine cream sauce with shallots, garlic, and thyme. Many French bistros served moules (moolz) with frites or french fries on the side. The mussels should all be slightly opened—don't eat the ones that are not. Pick up the mussel with your fingers, pry the shell the rest of the way open, use the oyster fork to grab it, swish it around in the broth, and eat. Some mussels might have escaped and are in the broth, so use your soup spoon to scoop and enjoy with the broth. You might also dip the bread in the broth. Served with an oyster fork, soup spoon, and discard bowl for the shells.

Mutton chop—(muh·tn chaap) is the chop that includes the loin and tenderloin from a mature sheep, usually served with fresh mint or mint jelly on the side. Mutton tends to be gamier than lamb because it is older. Served with a steak knife and fork.

Olives—(aa·luvz) when placed in a bowl or antipasto platter use your fingers to eat, if in a salad, use a fork. In all cases, the pit should be left on the side of your plate. Don't assume pits are out of every olive in salads or entrées, if a pit is left in by mistake, you can damage a tooth, so proceed with caution.

Oysters—(oy·strz) are a great way to start a meal and fun to share. Although they grow all over the world, you will usually see East Coast: Blue Point, Wellfleet, Island Creek, Beau Soleil, and West Coast: Kumamotos, Kusshi, Fanny Bay, and Nootka Sound to name a few. West Coast oysters are usually named after the location that they are from.

East Coast oysters tend to be brinier and saltier. West Coast oysters are smaller, plumper, milder, creamier, and sweeter with almost a nutty taste. The East Coast oysters have relatively flat shells while the West Coast shells are deeply fluted with sharp, pointed edges. I recommend ordering half East Coast and half West Coast, if available because the tastes are so different. It is fun to compare and can spur an interesting conversation and shared experience.

Oysters served on the half shell (raw) are usually sitting on a bed of crushed ice, accompanied by a piece of lemon, cocktail sauce, and sometimes a mignonette sauce (vinegar and shallots). If you are putting lemon on the whole serving, make sure you cover or shield the lemon when squeezing, so you don't squirt juice over those seated at the table. Some restaurants will put netting over the lemon to prevent it from spraying beyond the plate.

An oyster fork will be placed to the right of your knife. Hold the shell in your left hand and pierce the oyster with your oyster fork in your right hand. Put a bit of sauce on the oyster, pick up the shell, and use it to slide into your mouth, or use the oyster fork to lift them out and eat in one bite. Once finished, place the shell back on the crushed ice with the outer shell facing up.

Pasta—can be very easy to eat, but spaghetti or linguini may be challenging. Instead of going for the large spoon and fork to twirl, take just a few strands at a time and twirl on your fork. Do not cut pasta.

Many consider it inappropriate to add cheese to pasta with seafood. Seafood is considered to be delicate in flavor and cheese is strong, so the cheese might overpower the fish.

Pâté—(p·ah·tay) is finely chopped pork, liver or veal with fat, usually cooked in a terrine with herbs, spices, port or cognac. There are also seafood and vegetable pâtés. Pork pâté is usually served with a course mustard, or Dijon and cornichon pickles. A country pâté generally has a courser texture, and a mousse is lighter and easy to spread. Served with toast points or bread.

Pinza—(pin·zah) is a style of pizza with dough made of ancient Roman grains, so it is lighter in gluten and sugar, and more hydrated. The dough is pinched or poked, creating wonderful air pockets, crispy on the bottom, fluffy in the middle, and flaky on the top. I have been told that pinza is four hundred years older than pizza.

Pommes frites—(paam freet) long-cut french fries. French restaurants might serve with mayonnaise or mustard—try it, you might like it. Feel free to ask for ketchup.

Ragout—(ra·goo) is a thick highly seasoned meat stew.

Salmoriglio—(sal·more·eel·ee·yo) lemon juice, olive oil, garlic, salt, and herbs.

Seppia—(sep·pja) cuttlefish, of the squid or octopus family.

Shrimp cocktail—(shrimp kaak·tayl) are jumbo shrimp that are boiled, then chilled, and served with lemon and cocktail sauce. There are usually four to six in an order, depending on the size. If the shrimp is served with the tail still attached, use your fingers to eat it. You can also use an oyster fork or salad fork and knife if the shrimp are very large.

Soup—(soop) to hold the soup spoon, put your thumb on top of the handle and your index and middle finger underneath—think of holding a pencil. Scoop the soup away from you, then bring it to your mouth. The spoon should not be filled with more than 75 percent. Eat from the side, never placing the spoon entirely into your mouth. Put the soup spoon on the bottom plate holding the bowl when resting between bites. For that last taste, tilt the bowl away from you when scooping it up. Rest the spoon inside the bowl at 6:00 when finished.

Sous vide—(sou veed) is cooked in a vacuum-sealed pouch to keep the oxygen out while cooking to a very precise temperature.

Steak frites—(stayk freet) steak grilled and served with frites (french fries), usually served with herb butter, hollandaise or béarnaise sauce. The cut of beef varies, but it is usually a cut with some fat for flavor, and not usually a very thick cut. Served with a steak knife.

Steak tartare—(stayk tar·tar) is raw premium ground top sirloin mixed with raw egg yolk, onions, garlic, capers, Worcestershire sauce, ketchup, Dijon mustard, fresh pepper, and salt, with toast points on the side. Served with a fork and knife.

Sunchokes—(suhn·chohk) known as Jerusalem artichokes are starchy tubers like potatoes and turnips. They look like the choke or meaty part of the artichoke.

Sushi—(soo·shee) Japanese dish of bite-size pieces of fresh fish, egg or vegetable with rice. Not all sushi is raw; shrimp, softshell crab, lobster, and others may be cooked or cured. Sushi served without rice is called sashimi. Sushi wrapped in seaweed and cut into pieces is Maki, and wrapped as a handroll that looks like a cone is Temaki.

Sushi has its own set of rules, and I highly suggest delving deeper into proper etiquette. Here are just a few highlights:

- Some say sushi should only be eaten with your fingers, and sashimi with chopsticks.
- Ginger is not eaten with or on sushi; it is eaten between bites as a palate cleanser.
- Wasabi should be gently placed on top of the fish if you need it. Do not mix it with the soy sauce.
- If soy sauce is added, it should be added to the top of the fish, not the rice—this is easy to do with your hands. If using chopsticks, it is best to have one chopstick on the top or fish side, and one on the bottom, then turn so just the fish is touching the soy sauce.
- Do not shake the sushi after adding soy sauce, that is considered to be rude.

Tahini—(tuh·hee·nee) is a ground sesame paste, or butter made of sesame seeds, oil, and salt.

Tapas—(taa·puhz) are Spanish small plates of olives, cheese, and plates of cured meats. Some hot tapas dishes may include fried anchovies, eggplant, shrimp, and chorizo.

Tapenade—(taa·puh·naa·duh) is a spread or dip made from kalamata olives, red onion, roasted garlic, capers, Dijon mustard, red wine vinegar, chili flakes, and olive oil.

Toast points—usually white toast that has the crust cut off and cut diagonally into four pieces. The diagonal cut creates a triangle shape. Toast points are served with pâte, steak tartare, cheese, and other appetizers.

Truffles—(truh·flz) are very expensive fungi that grow in the shadow of oak and hazelnut trees. Although found throughout the world, rich black truffles are generally grown in France and white truffles in Italy. They have a deep musky aroma, and some say a slightly garlicky flavor. Pungent but subtle, they are known to enhance savory dishes as well as sweet. Because the taste can be so strong, people seem to love them or prefer to pass. Truffles are often used in sauces, infused into oils, or grated over pasta.

When adding truffles to a dish, think butter, cream, and earthy foods as well as steak and chicken. It is best to stay away from tomatoes, acidic foods, and fish.

White and black truffles should not be confused with dessert truffles or chocolate truffles, which is a chocolate candy made with a layer of ganache, chocolate, and cream.

Tuna Nicoise—(tu·nuh nee·swaaz) is a French-style tuna salad. If the tuna is sushi-grade, it will be pan-seared, and cooked to order, with a recommendation of rare or medium-rare. Some restaurants use canned tuna, packed in oil, so best to ask. Other ingredients are usually hard-boiled egg, boiled potato, haricot vert, cucumber, tomatoes, Boston Bibb, anchovies, olives, capers, extra virgin olive oil, lemon juice, salt, and pepper. It might be served with a steak knife if sushi-grade, if not, a fork and knife.

Tuna tartare—raw tuna cut into small pieces and seasoned with Asian flavors of ginger, soy, lime juice, chilies, sesame seeds, and other herbs such as chives and cilantro.

Zeppole—(zeh·puh·lee) fried donut balls made out of cream puff dough. They can be savory or sweet.

FINGER FOOD

Artichokes

Asparagus—when served on a separate plate with a dipping sauce.

Bacon—when crisp and served whole.

Burrito

Caviar—when served on a toast point, mini-blini or cracker.

Corn on the cob—eat just a few rows at a time, served with butter and salt.

French fries

Fried chicken

Olives

Pickles

Pizza—unless it is messy or has lots of toppings.

Raw bar—oysters, clams, mussels, and shrimp.

Sushi

Tacos

PASTA SHAPES

Agnolotti—(ah·nyuh·laht·tee) half-moon rectangles filled with meat, cheese or vegetables.

Bucatini—(boo·kuh·tee·nee) is long and thin like spaghetti with a hole in the center.

Cannelloni—(kan·uh·low·nee) short wide tubes.

Capellini—(cah·peh·lee·nee) angel hair, the thinnest, most delicate long strands.

Cappelletti—(cah·peh·lay·tee) are little hats stuffed with cheese filling.

Cascatelli—(caska·telli) is a 3-D C made of an open tube with ribbon ruffles protruding out on each side of the outer rim of the half circle to capture the sauce.

Conchiglie—(con·keel·yay) shells.

Farfalle—(far·fall·lay) bow tie shaped.

Fettuccine—(fay·tuh·chee·nee) long flat ribbons.

Fusilli—(foo·zee·lee) spiral-shaped–rotini is similar.

Gnocchi—(nyow·kee) dumplings made of potatoes.

Linguini—(lin·gwee·nee) long strands not as flat as fettuccini.

Orecchiette—(oh·reck·ET·tay) earlike shape.

Pappardelle—(pa·par·day·lay) is the widest and flattest ribbon pasta.

Penne—(peh·neh) tubular with the ends cut on an angle (think pencil).

Radiatori—(ra·di·a·toree) ruffled and ridged, think little radiators.

Rigatoni—(rig·uh·toe·nee) large, short tubes with ridges on the sides.

Spaghetti—(spuh·geh·tee) long thin strands.

Tagliatelle—(tah·lyah·tell·eh) egg pasta, long thin strands like fettuccine.

Tortellini—(tore·tuh·lee·nee) are like little hats filled with meat, cheese, or vegetables.

Vermicelli—(ver·mih·chell·ee) thin strands like capellini broken into short pieces.

Ziti—(zee·tee) medium-size tubular pasta.

Chapter 20

FISH

Most fish served in restaurants is farm-raised. If wild-caught it is caught in the wild and should offer a rich, fresh taste. There are many types of fish as well as ways to prepare them. The easiest thing to remember is the whiter the flesh of the fish, the milder it is. If you are looking for a fish that doesn't taste fishy, I recommend a white fish such as branzino or sole.

MILD-tasting fish is usually white fish with low oil content. Prepared in most ways such as sautéed, poached, pan-seared, and baked. It can also be grilled as a whole fish.

- Branzino
- Catfish
- Cod (flaky)
- Haddock
- Halibut (steaks or filets)
- Monkfish (meaty/moderate oil)
- Skate (firm, chewy)
- Sole
- Tilapia
- Yellowtail

MEDIUM-flavored is usually firm and prepared in all ways including grilled.

- Chilian sea bass

- Grouper
- Snapper
- Swordfish
- Trout

FULL-flavored fish is usually dark flesh, with heavier natural oil content, with a flavor of their own. They can be prepared stovetop, in the oven, or on a grill.

- Arctic char (trout like, but think salmon)
- Bluefish (cook with lemon to cut the oil)
- Mahimahi (firm, meaty, slightly fishy)
- Mackerel
- Salmon (Coho, Sockeye, Atlantic)
- Tuna (firm, great for grilling)

SAUCES FOR FISH

Béchamel—(bay·shah·mehl) white sauce with herbs. The base is made from a roux of flour, milk, and butter.

Beurre blanc—(burr blahn) white butter sauce: white wine, vinegar, shallots, and butter.

Beurre noir—(burr nwar) brown butter, capers, lemon, and parsley.

Hollandaise—(haa·luhn·dayz) egg yolks emulsified with clarified butter, lemon, and a pinch of cayenne and salt.

Mornay—(mor·nay) is a béchamel with cheese.

Salmoriglio sauce—(sal·more·eel·ee·yo) lemon juice, olive oil, garlic, salt, and herbs.

Tomato sauce—(tuh·may·tow saas) is made with crushed tomatoes, onion, parsley, garlic, and sometimes cream.

SAUCES FOR SHELLFISH

Cocktail sauce—(kaak·tayl) ketchup and horseradish.

Mignonette—(min·yuh·net) vinegar, shallots, and sometimes red pepper flakes.

Pink mayonnaise—(may·un·naz) mayonnaise, a dash of ketchup, Tabasco, sherry, and sometimes tarragon.

Chapter 21

BEEF

STEAK HOUSES OFFER SEVERAL CUTS of beef that may be as small as three ounces up to forty ounces, or even larger. The cuts of beef differ widely in how marbleized it is, meaning the amount of fat, the thickness, and whether it is served on the bone or not. This section discusses the more popular cuts of beef with a description and sauces that might be served with them.

Chateaubriand—(shaa·tow·bree·aand) is a beef tenderloin roast. It is usually made to serve two or more. When ordering in a restaurant, it may be accompanied by side dishes including a potato, vegetables, and a sauce. This usually takes about forty minutes to cook for medium-rare, so it should be ordered promptly. Served with a steak knife and serving utensils.

Côte de boeuf—(coat·d·buff) bone-in rib eye is usually prepared for two or more. It has all the marbling and fat that offers an incredible flavor. It takes a solid forty minutes to cook medium-rare, so keep that in mind when ordering. Côte de boeuf is usually served with sides and a sauce. Served with a steak knife and serving utensils.

Filet mignon—(fuh·lay muhn·yaan) is known as beef tenderloin, which is considered the height of richness. It is the most tender of all cuts of beef, known for its delicate, butter-like texture, so tender you can cut it with a butter knife. A béarnaise or hollandaise sauce may accompany it. Served with a steak knife.

Kobe beef—(kow·bee) is a type of Wagyu known as one of the highest-quality meats in the world. It is known for its flavor, marbling, and texture. It is incredibly rich, buttery, and smooth.

New York strip—is particularly tender and does not include the bone. It is leaner than a rib eye but with more fat than a filet or tenderloin. Served with a steak knife.

Prime rib—is cut from the prime area along the rib cage. This cut is roasted whole and then sliced into thick pieces. Prime rib requires hours of cooking, so it is usually served at restaurants known for their prime rib or on special occasions. Many serve with a jus and a horseradish sauce on the side. Served with a steak knife.

Porterhouse steak—is a larger version of the T-bone steak, specifically with a larger section of filet or tenderloin. According to the USDA, it must be at least one-and-a-quarter inches thick. Served with a steak knife.

Rib eye steak—has a nice marbling and a fatty cap, which makes it more tender and flavorful. If you want a very flavorful steak without the high-fat content then go with the strip. If going for flavor at all costs, go with the rib eye. Served with a steak knife.

T-bone steak—is easy to identify with a T-shaped bone in the center. On one side you have the strip steak, and the other side is tenderloin or filet mignon. Served with a steak knife.

Wagyu beef—(waa·gyoo) is a breed of Japanese cattle. Wagyu beef is extremely rich in monosaturated fatty acids and has the most outstanding marbling scores in the world. Wagyu offers more flavor, and it is incredibly tender and juicy. Served with a steak knife.

PREPARATION

When you order a steak, the server will ask how you would like it prepared. As the meat cooks, it loses moisture, becoming firmer and drier, so the chef's recommendation is normally to order it medium-rare. This is also why some kitchens refuse to cook steak beyond medium-well. Cooking steak that much masks the flavor and textural profile. If that's how you like it, that's how you like it, but that's the reason people may judge the order, so maybe bear that in mind when dining with new colleagues.

Regardless of your meat preparation preference, at a restaurant each term refers to a specific temperature. The kitchen must ensure they prepare meat safely and properly, and that they do not waste costly food items. That's why the kitchen relies on meat thermometers to confirm the food is ready. But just because the chef knows it is cooked as requested, doesn't mean it meets the customer's expectations. If you're unsure how you like it, or have very specific preferences, describe visually what you want to make sure you're speaking the same language.

Medium-rare is seared on the outside, warm and red in the center. It's cooked just long enough to enhance the flavor, but the meat retains its tenderness and is usually very juicy. 130-135 degrees Fahrenheit.

Medium is also seared on the outside, but there is a pink rim around a dash of red in the center, it will be a bit firmer than medium-rare and still quite flavorful. 140-145 degrees Fahrenheit.

Well-done should not have any pink in the middle. There is a chance it might be a little tough or chewy because it has lost most of its moisture. 170 degrees Fahrenheit.

Tip: if you must order a steak well-done, you might order it butterflied, giving the kitchen permission to cut the meat allowing more surface to be exposed to the heat, for a faster cook time. This should also result in a more well-done piece of meat.

SAUCES FOR MEAT

Au poivre—(oh·pwa·vruh) butter, olive oil, peppercorns, cognac, heavy cream, and kosher salt.

Béarnaise—(bā-är·nāz) egg yolks emulsified with clarified butter, white wine vinegar, shallots, and tarragon.

Bordelaise—(bawr·dl·eyz) beef stock, sherry vinegar, shallots, thyme, parsley, bay leaf, peppercorns, dry red wine, and kosher salt.

Chimichurri—(chim·ee·choor·ee) finely chopped parsley, thyme, garlic, oregano, white wine vinegar, olive oil, and kosher salt.

Hollandaise—(haa·luhn·dayz) egg yolks emulsified with clarified butter, lemon, a pinch of cayenne, and kosher salt.

Hotel butter—a combination of butter, garlic, shallots, parsley, thyme, lemon, kosher salt, and pepper. It is usually served as a chilled pat of butter on top of a steak (steak frites), so it slowly melts in.

Red wine jus—(zhyou) port, red wine, shallots, chicken stock, orange zest, coriander, thyme, black pepper, and kosher salt.

Chapter 22

CHEESE, DESSERT, COFFEE, AND TEA

ALTHOUGH IT IS MORE COMMON to have dessert or a sweet following a meal, a cheese plate sometimes accompanied by a sherry or port is another fine choice.

CHEESE PLATE

Everything on the plate is there for a reason. The chef and their team spend hours thinking of the right combination, pairing tastes, textures, and aesthetics to wow you. A cheese plate that made an impression on me was at Augustine, a beautiful Keith McNally restaurant, in downtown New York City. Marcus Glocker was the chef, and everything that came out of his kitchen was exquisite. The cheese was Brillat-Savarin, accompanied by slivers of Granny Smith apple, pieces of dried fruit, a mint garnish, delicately drizzled with honey, and served with toasted sourdough bread. The presentation was so elegant, on a small, flowered plate. It was the first time I ever tried honey on cheese. How had no one ever told me about this before? The cheese, a triple cream, was amazing. It has become a staple at my parties—served with honey, of course.

When putting together a cheese plate with multiple types of cheese, it is nice to select them from different categories. One way to differentiate is:

- Aged: cheddar, Gouda, and Gruyère
- Bold: blue, Gorgonzola, Roquefort, Stilton
- Firm: Edam, Manchego, and parmigiano
- Soft: Brie, Camembert or goat cheese

Murray's Cheese on Bleecker Street in Greenwich Village has taught me so much about cheese over the years. I always look forward to my jaunt downtown to shop there. Their staff is incredibly knowledgeable and welcoming—making for an ultimate NYC experience.

Often, I will take Murray's descriptions that come with the cheese, type them out, and place them next to the cheese on the cheese board so everyone knows what they are eating. It can also help start a dialogue about the cheese and pairings, which can be fun, as well as informative.

I like to finish a cheese board with charcuterie meats such as mortadella, coppa, and chorizo. Along with Castelvetrano olives, Red Anjou or Bartlett pear, grapes, walnuts, and apricot or fig spread.

When cheese is served to share, there are different knives for cutting and serving the different cheeses, so try not to mix them up. When served cheese in a restaurant or eating it without bread, it should be with a dessert fork and knife. Fromage is cheese in French and formaggio in Italian.

DESSERT

Baklava—(baa·kluh·vaa) a small pastry made of phyllo pastry dough filled with chopped nuts and sweetened with honey and syrup.

Chocolate mousse—(moos) light and fluffy and made of chocolate, cream, sugar, eggs, and butter.

Cobbler—(kob·ler) deep-dish single-crusted fruit pie, the crust is usually on top, made with a sweet rich biscuit dough, filled with fruit.

Crème brûlée—(krem broo·ley) a rich vanilla custard with caramelized sugar on top that is hardened with a torch flame.

Crepe—(krayp) a paper-thin pancake that can be filled with fruit, creams, cheese or savory ingredients. They are sometimes topped with whipped cream.

Crostata—(kru·staa·tah) rustic open tart, usually fruit-filled, similar to a galette.

Flan—(flaan) from Spain, known as crème caramel—egg custard baked in a mold with caramel sauce at the bottom. It is turned upside down when served.

Galette—(guh·let) flat crust made with pastry or bread dough covered with sugar, pastry cream or a thin layer of fruit. It has a rustic look, like a dessert pizza.

Gelato—(jah·laa·tow) the Italian name for ice cream. The base is made with milk, cream, sugar, and sometimes eggs.

Ice cream—(ise kreem) a wonderful combination of milk, cream, sugar, eggs, and sometimes fresh fruit or nuts.

Linzer torte—(lin·zr tort) is a lattice-top tart made with a rich crumbly nut crust and filled with raspberry jam.

Mille-feuille—(mil·foy) classic Napoleon—three layers of puff pastry coated with a berry jam and filled with vanilla pastry cream.

Pavlova—(paav·low·vuh) baked meringue filled with lemon mascarpone mousse and yogurt, topped with warm seasonal berries.

Profiteroles—(pruh·fit·uh·roh) are small puff pastry balls filled with vanilla ice cream and covered with a warm chocolate ganache or syrup.

Sherbet—(shur·buht) usually has dairy and is filled with fruit juice, honey, and other sugar-sweetened tastes.

Sorbet—(sor·bay) more like fine ice but very smooth and is generally dairy free.

Soufflé—(soo·flay) a light and fluffy egg-based dessert that originated in France. It is usually light and airy and rises inches above the dish it is baked in. Because it could take twenty to thirty minutes to bake it is usually recommended to order it when you place your entrée order.

Tarte tatin—(tart tuh·tan) classic French upside-down caramelized apple tart. Named after the Tartin sisters who served it at their hotel in Loire Valley, France.

Torte—(tort) a multilayered, rich cake that is filled with whipped cream, buttercream, mousses, fruit, or jams.

Tiramisu—(tir·uh·mee·soo) ladyfingers soaked in espresso and brandy or Kahlua, slathered with lightly sweetened whipped cream mascarpone.

COFFEE

Americano—espresso topped with hot water.

Cappuccino—a double shot of espresso with mostly foamy steamed milk.

Coffee—American coffee.

Espresso—Italian roast–single or double.

Espresso con panna—espresso topped with whipped cream.

Espresso macchiato—single espresso topped with a small amount of steamed foamy milk.

Latte—a double shot of espresso topped with lightly foamy milk.

TEA

Assam—Indian black teas, malty, full-bodied.

Chai—fragrant spices blended with Indian Assam tea (black tea).

Chamomile—calming, flower petals, with honey notes.

Darjeeling—Indian black tea, with a delicate flavor.

Earl Grey—black flavored tea with a citrus scent.

English breakfast—strong malty tea from India (black tea).

Irish breakfast—bolder than English breakfast, robust, and rich black tea.

Jasmine Pearl—flower-scented classic Chinese green tea.

Lemon verbena—fragrant leaves with an intense citrus flavor.

Orange spice—black tea scented with orange and spice.

Peppermint—aromatic, sweet, and soothing.

HOT BEVERAGE ALTERNATIVES

Fresh lemon in hot water.

Fresh mint leaves in hot water, lemon or lime wedge add a nice taste.

Chapter 23

COCKTAIL NOTES

COCKTAILS ARE VERY MUCH IN vogue and many restaurants have unique cocktails curated by a mixologist along with bartenders who are familiar with making all types of drinks. Cocktails might include fresh juices, fermentations, infusions, bitters, and herbs along with the various spirits that are used as their base.

Most mixed drinks like a gin and tonic or vodka and soda contain one shot of gin or vodka, which is generally one and a half ounces. A cocktail such as a martini or Manhattan contains two to three ounces of alcohol.

When ordering a spirit such as scotch or bourbon, if you don't want it with a mixer, you will order it neat, without ice, or on the rocks, with ice.

ICE

Ice comes in many sizes and shapes, and each has an impact on the taste of the drink. Dry ice or a specially created ice cube is sometimes used for aesthetic purposes.

A memorable ice cube for me was in a White Cosmopolitan I ordered at Daniel in New York City. It was described as an "orchid suspended within a sphere of ice." The orchid was frozen within a round ice cube, and as the ice melted the orchid lay on top of the cocktail. It was both beautiful and delicious.

Bruised ice—When a cocktail is shaken with ice, that ice is considered bruised or broken down. That ice is discarded, and the cocktail will be strained or poured into a fresh glass with fresh ice that will not melt as quickly as the bruised ice, so as to not dilute the cocktail.

Crushed ice—This ice dilutes as part of the mixing process. Crushed ice is usually used for mint juleps and Moscow mules.

Dirty ice—When a martini is ordered up with dirty ice on the side, the ice the martini was shaken with (dirty ice) will be served on the side, in a rocks glass.

Dry ice—The solid form of carbon dioxide that is sometimes used for aesthetic purposes. When mixed in a drink it will bubble and create a fog that lifts from the top of the cocktail. The dry ice will sink to the bottom of the glass and melt within four or five minutes. You should not touch or swallow the dried ice, but it is perfectly safe in your drink.

Large cube—The large cube melts more slowly than the traditional one-inch cube, which shares more surface with the liquor, therefore diluting it. The large cube helps keep the integrity of the spirit or drink longer while keeping it chilled.

THE GARNISH

A garnish makes the drink look more pleasing aesthetically, enhances the taste, and may add a refreshing scent. The traditional garnishes are:

- Cherry for a Manhattan
- Grapefruit slice for a Paloma
- Lemon or lime wedges for most vodka, gin or tequila drinks
- Orange slice or twist for a negroni
- Small onions for a Gibson
- Twist or olive for a martini

When a citrus twist is squeezed or twisted, a slight oil essence comes from the rind, which adds to the taste of the drink. If a wedge or slice is added, the juice from the fruit adds a freshness to both the taste and smell.

When mixologists elevated the traditional cocktails, new garnishes were added as well. It is now common to see fresh mint, rosemary, sage, cinnamon, lavender, cucumber slices, and jalapeno slices as a garnish.

Misters or atomizers are also used to start or finish a cocktail with a specific flavor. If starting the cocktail, you can mist a slight coat on the inside of the glass before adding the mixed drink. If finishing a drink you might mist the top, so the first smell will be of the essence, as the taste of the drink then comes through.

SHAKEN NOT STIRRED

I remember hearing James Bond ordering his martini shaken, not stirred. Although most bartenders make them that way for efficiency and demonstrative reasons, the proper way of making a martini is by stirring it, not shaking it, so it is smoother and not diluted.

Cocktails with juice, egg or cream are usually shaken so the different textures blend evenly for a consistent taste. Cocktails that are spirit-forward, or boozy as I call them, are usually stirred.

MUDDLED

Old-fashioneds and Moscow mules come to my mind when I think of a muddled cocktail. The fruit, sugar, and herbs are gingerly broken down with a rounded wooden spoon or blunt muddle to infuse the flavors, then the spirits are added.

Some insist that fine herbs like mint or basil should be slapped so the oils are awakened, but the leaf is not bruised. Since mint can become bitter if muddled, I can only guess that because so much mint is used in a mojito, which is muddled, the bruised leaves are outnumbered by the fresh, so the bitterness is not the taste that comes forward.

Chapter 24

COCKTAIL GLASSES AND RECIPES

Collins   Hi-Ball   Rocks   Martini   Nick & Nora   Coupe   Snifter   Shot glass

GLASS SHAPES AND SIZES HAVE changed over the years but usually have a reason for their shape. The shape of red wine glasses and snifters helps to capture and enhance the bouquet of the beverage. White wine glasses and flutes are narrower, so they help preserve the aroma, maintain the cool temperature, and enable the effervescence to last longer.

Collins and highball glasses are for mixed drinks over ice. Offering a taller glass is great for more than one mixer, making for a lighter cocktail. The slenderer glass also helps retain carbonation.

Old-fashioned glasses are for boozy cocktails on the rocks like a Manhattan or old-fashioned, or for a spirit served neat, like bourbon or rye.

The coupe, Nick and Nora, and martini glasses are perfect for cocktails served up. The stem allows you to hold the drink without impacting the temperature. And the shape offers plenty of room for an elaborate garnish leaving plenty of room to sip from.

- **Collins**—also known as a tumbler.
- **Highball**—taller than an old-fashioned glass, shorter than a collins glass.
- **Double old-fashioned glass**—known as a rock, lowball or short tumbler.
- **Martini glass**—long stem with cone-shaped bowl, holds eight ounces or more.
- **Nick and Nora**—four to six ounces, long stem, high sides, and narrow bowl; a small martini glass.
- **Coupe**—the original Champagne glass offers a nice size stem to hold so your hand doesn't warm the drink. The glass is great for cocktails served up, with its nice wide mouth, holds four to six ounces.
- **Snifter**—has a very large bowl that tightens at the top to hold the aroma. The large bowl is perfect for swirling.
- **Shot glass**—usually one and a half ounces.

BASIC COCKTAIL RECIPES

Cosmopolitan
2 oz. vodka
1 oz. 100 percent cranberry juice
1/2 oz. Cointreau
1/2 oz. lime juice
1 tsp simple or maple syrup
1 lime wedge as garnish
Serve in a chilled martini glass

French Martini
1.5 oz. vodka
1/2 oz. Chambord
3/4 oz. pineapple juice
Shake well with ice
Serve in a chilled martini glass

French 75
3 oz. Champagne
1 oz. gin or cognac
1/2 oz. simple syrup
1/4 oz. lemon juice
Shake well with ice
Strain into a flute

Margarita
1.5 oz. tequila
1 oz. Cointreau or triple sec
3/4 oz. fresh lime juice
Kosher salt on the rim
Lime wedge as a garnish
Up or rocks: salted rim

Negroni
1 oz. gin
1 oz. Campari
1 oz. sweet vermouth
Orange slice or twist
Serve on the rocks

Martini
2 ½ oz. gin or vodka
1/2 oz. dry vermouth
Shake well with ice
Serve up in a martini glass or on the rocks
Lemon twist or olive
Dirty is with olive juice

Old-fashioned
2 oz. rye or bourbon
2-4 dashes of bitters
1 sugar cube
1 orange peel
1/2 teaspoon water
Serve on the rocks

Manhattan
2 oz. bourbon or rye
1/2 oz. sweet vermouth
2 dashes of bitters
Shake well with ice
Strain into a chilled martini glass (up) or on the rocks
Cherry garnish

Espresso Martini
2 oz. vodka or vanilla vodka
1/2 oz. Kahlua or coffee liquor
1 oz. cold espresso
1/2 oz. simple syrup
Shake well with ice, then strain into chilled a martini glass
Garnish: 3 espresso beans

Chapter 25

THE WINE GUIDE

ALTHOUGH I LOVED MY JOB waitering at One Fifth, when I saw my peers get promoted to wine captain, I knew I wanted to pursue that as well. Realizing I needed to expand my knowledge of wines, I approached Phil Nugent, the beverage manager, and asked if he would teach us if I put together a group. Although he agreed, he was leery of the staff's interest.

Phil was delighted to see every waiter show up, eager to learn the list and taste the wines so they would be able to highlight and discuss the wines with our patrons. He was so excited that at the end of the first class, he asked us to wait a few minutes. He ran into the kitchen and asked them to cut up some honeydew melon. He pulled a bottle of Chateau d'Yquem, rated the best Sauterne in the world.

Phil said, "This is my gift to you." He poured a taste for everyone.

"Take a sip, wait, now take a bite of the melon." Not only was the wine incredible, but it taught us the power of the perfect pairing of wine and food. After having the melon, the taste of the wine came back ever so faintly. It was an incredible sensation.

I am proud to say I was One Fifth's first female wine captain (1980). As a wine captain, I was the liaison between our wines and the guests. Additionally, I was responsible for overall service. Now most fine restaurants hold mandatory training to ensure their staff is familiar with their wines, food, and beverages.

My wine comments are from what I have learned over the years. The restaurants that I worked in concentrated on wines from France, Italy, and Northern California, so that is what I am presenting. But there are outstanding wines produced all over the world, so please be open to them, and try them. This is meant as an overview, enough for you to be knowledgeable, comfortable, and confident as you begin your restaurant and dining journey. I highly recommend buying a book or two and looking for tastings that you might enjoy.

We begin with a few terms that are frequently used, then grapes and wines from France, Italy, and California.

WINE TERMS

Acidity—the balance between fruit and acid and is important to the aging process.

Aging—the step between fermentation and bottling and has been done for years in barrels. An average aging time can be six to thirty months. Some red wines are aged for many years. Different kinds and sizes of barrels offer different flavors such as woody, vanilla, or coconut. Oak barrels are probably the most common barrels for red wines and Chardonnay. Oxygen comes through the oak barrel to help age it and tannins help develop structure over time.

Fermentation—the formula sugar + yeast = alcohol + carbon dioxide. The yeast consumes the sugars in the grape and produces alcohol and carbon dioxide, which is crucial in creating aromas and tastes in wine.

Tannin—a natural preservative that adds to the wine's longevity. Tannin is not a taste; it is a tactile sensation that is more prevalent in red wine than in white wine.

Terroir—refers to the environment where wine is produced. The region, sunlight, climate, rainfall, drainage, and nearby plants are instrumental to the "taste of the soil." The soil can include slate, chalk, limestone, clay, sandstone, granite, schist, and shale.

Stainless steel tanks are used mainly for white wine. They don't allow oxygen in, so the wines are generally clean and crisp. Chardonnay that is aged in oak will be heavier and more intense than those aged in stainless steel (Chablis.) Concrete barrels are also used. Concrete is porous, so it allows oxygen to come in through the clay, producing silky smooth wines.

WINE BOTTLE SHAPE

Several traditional bottle shapes trace back to the wine's origin.

Burgundy—wider bottom with sloping shoulders.

Bordeaux—straight with high shoulders.

Alsace—tall and slender.

Sparkling—thicker glass with sloping shoulders and punt in the bottom for strength.

Port—straight with high shoulders, some have a bulb in the neck to catch sediment.

Ice or dessert—straight, thin, high-shouldered, elegant, usually half the volume of wine.

Chapter 26

FRENCH WINES

FRENCH WINEMAKERS ESTABLISHED TRADITIONS AND rules for making wine centuries ago and for the most part, they have gone unchanged. AOC (Appellation d'Origine Contrôlée) is the official French wine classification, which refers to geographical origin and quality. Due to strict regulations, French wines offer consistency so you should find it easier to identify the taste with the region and grape. The French wine regions are Champagne, Loire Valley, Alsace, Bordeaux, Burgundy, Rhône, Languedoc, Provence, and Corsica.

MAJOR GRAPES BY REGION

WHITE WINE

- **Bordeaux**—Sauvignon Blanc and Semillon
- **Chablis and Burgundy**—Chardonnay
- **Loire Valley**—Muscadet, Chenin Blanc, and Sauvignon Blanc

RED WINE

- **Bordeaux**—Cabernet Sauvignon, Merlot, and Cabernet Franc
- **Burgundy**—Pinot Noir
- **Rhône**—Syrah and Grenache

Although there are many different grapes, my recommendation is to sample the major varieties and learn their origin and taste and see which you prefer. After years of trying to figure out French wines, I found that looking at a map and following the grapes by region made it much easier to understand and remember.

FRANCE

Champagne is located in north-central France. Champagne is made from Pinot Noir, Chardonnay, and Pinot Meunier. Directly below is Chablis that is 100 percent Chardonnay (white). Loire to the farthest west has Muscadet made from Melon de Bourgogne grape. In the eastern part of Loire, below Chablis is home to Sancerre and Pouilly-Fumé, both 100 percent Sauvignon Blanc. Burgundy on the eastern side is primarily Chardonnay for white wines and Pinot Noir for red wines. Nestled between Burgundy and Rhône is Beaujolais, 100 percent Gamay. South of Burgundy is Rhône, home of Syrah and Grenache; the primary grapes for Châteauneuf-du-Pape (there are thirteen) and Gigondas. On the western part of the country below the Loire Valley is Bordeaux, which produces Cabernet Sauvignon, Cabernet Franc, Merlot, Semillon, and Sauvignon Blanc.

WINE GEOGRAPHICALLY

CHAMPAGNE

Champagne is the ultimate, elegant, premier sparkling wine. Dry with high acidity, citrus, green fruit flavors, and subtle hints of almond and brioche. Champagne is located in the northeastern part of France. It is the only place in the world where Champagne can be made. The summers are short, the winters are cold and gray, and the soil is chalk and limestone.

Champagne is made from Chardonnay, Pinot Noir, and Pinot Meunier. Blanc de Blanc is from white grapes and Blanc de Noir is from black grapes. The sweetness level varies depending on the amount of sugar added in the final stages of the winemaking.

The process of making Champagne is known as méthode champenoise. In the first fermentation, yeast is added to convert the grape's sugars to alcohol. In the second fermentation, the still wine and a mixture of sugar and yeast are bottled under a temporary crown cap and stored horizontally. Contact with the dead yeast cells, known as lees, enhances the sparkling wine's flavor, usually bringing in hints of brioche and almond. Blending grapes allow winemakers to create a taste that best represents their "house style."

It is the yeast that slowly converts the sugar to alcohol and creates CO_2, the bubbles. The bottles are put on special racks that hold them with the neck of the bottle downward at a forty-five-degree angle. The bottles are turned every so often so the lees will settle at the neck of the bottle.

Once this process is complete, the temporary crown cap is removed to disgorge the dead yeast and sediment. Some freeze the neck of the bottle for easier removal. The lost liquid is replaced by still wine and sugar, which determines the wine's level of sweetness. The final cork and wire cage are then placed on the bottle.

Méthode charmat is another way of making some sparkling wines. Pressurized vats are used in the fermenting process versus individual bottles. Wines don't necessarily pick up the same richness as the wines that ferment with the lees in individual bottles but are still lovely.

Champagne not only brings a celebratory feel to any event, but it is also incredibly versatile, pairing with just about any type or style of food, from triple cream brie, caviar, oysters, fish, steak, fried chicken, and vegetable dishes. Champagne is a perfect complement.

SPARKLING WINES

Crémant is a sparkling wine made the same way as Champagne and is produced throughout France, using the grapes synonymous with the region. Since they, too, have the second fermentation in a bottle versus large vats, they have a richness similar to Champagne but at a much lower price point.

Champagne and Crémant are fermented in the bottle, as is Cava, a sparkling wine from Spain. Prosecco, Italy's sparkling wine uses the charmat process resulting in a fresh and fruity wine that doesn't necessarily have the toastiness of those aging on lees in individual bottles. Prosecco is usually sweeter than Crémant or Cava, with apple, honeysuckle, peach, melon, and pear flavors.

THE LOIRE VALLEY

The Loire Valley is on the northwest side of France; it runs the length of the Loire River. It is known for its white wines, ranging from dry to sweet, crafted in a lighter style due to the region's cooler climate. Muscadet, named for the region is lean, and green, with an almost saline-like quality. It is made from the Melon de Bourgogne grape. It is closest to the sea and pairs beautifully with oysters and shellfish. Sancerre, one of the most recognizable appellations for French Sauvignon Blanc in the Loire Valley offers a more medium-bodied wine, ripe gooseberry aromas, and flinty-smoke flavors. Pouilly-Fumé, the most concentrated wine of Loire Valley, is 100 percent Sauvignon Blanc grape. It is rivaled in this regard only by Sancerre, just the other side of the Loire River, and Vouvray, from the Chenin Blanc grape.

ALSACE

Alsace is on the eastern border between France and Germany. It is known for its elegant dry Riesling wines, off-dry Pinot Gris, and full-bodied Gewürztraminer. The wines are lean and refreshing with floral and peachy notes and vibrant acidity. Alsace names its wines by grape varietal instead of a place of origin. About 90 percent of the wines produced there are white wines. They pair well with salty hams, sausages, spiced foods, shellfish, egg dishes, and white meat.

BORDEAUX

For the International Exposition of 1855, wine brokers were asked to select the best wines that represented France. The brokers agreed with the provision if it were never to become official. They ranked the top Médoc wines according to price, which correlated to quality at the time. The top four, now five vineyards, or crus produced "first growth" wines; the next fourteen made second growth, and this continued through fifth-growth producers. First growth doesn't mean the first vines ever, it refers to the first class of wines. Much of this classification system has remained the same. In 1920, Baron Philippe de Rothschild challenged his château as a second growth, and after years, in 1973 it was awarded first-growth status.

Some of the best wines in the world are from Bordeaux, France. The Gironde estuary divides the Bordeaux region into the left and right banks. The left and right banks both combine Cabernet Sauvignon, Merlot, and Cabernet Franc for their red wines. One thing to remember is the left bank wines usually have at least 50 percent Cabernet Sauvignon and the right bank wines at least 50 percent Merlot. Eighty-five percent of the wine produced in Bordeaux is red.

Four regions that stand out are Médoc, Graves/Pessac-Léognan, Pomerol, and Saint Emilion. Médoc has seven subsidiary appellations: Saint-Estèphe, Pauillac, Saint-Julien, Margaux, Haut-Médoc, Listrac-Médoc, and Moulis-en-Médoc, all on the left bank. The left bank is made up of dry, deep rocky soils that are good for growing Cabernet Sauvignon, the dominant grape on the west bank.

Saint Estèphe is the farthest north appellation and is considered the "most masculine" as the soils are very deep and take longer for the grape to ripen. Margaux is considered the softest and more delicate. Saint Julien vines sit on a deep bed of sedimentary rock so the wines there may vary more. Pauillac is the most representative of the region and includes three of the five premier crus. Pauillac has the highest elevation on the left bank, gravelly soils with a nearby forest that helps protect the vines from harsh winds. South of Bordeaux, the left bank includes Pessac-Léognan and Graves.

The right bank has dry clay soils that are perfect for Merlot and Cabernet Franc. The right bank uses at least 50 percent Merlot in their wine, so they are traditionally smoother with a silky finish versus the earthier left bank wines. Pomerol and Saint Emilion are in the right bank.

1855 classification were all from Médoc except for Château Haut-Brion from Graves:

- Château Haut-Brion, Pessac, AOC Pessac-Léognan
- Château Lafite Rothschild, Pauillac, AOC Pauillac
- Château Latour, Pauillac, AOC Pauillac
- Château Margaux, Margaux, AOC Margaux
- Château Mouton Rothschild, Pauillac, AOC Pauillac

Wines from the left bank go beautifully with just about any grilled, braised or roasted meat, beef, veal, pork, duck, and game. They also complement roast chicken, mushrooms, truffles, and other earthy types of foods. The wines from the right bank also pair well with beef, game, chicken, veal, pork, fish, and cheese.

White wines from Bordeaux tend to be light and fruity with citrus flavors and aromas of flowers and fresh-cut grass. Semillon adds a touch of complexity that can sometimes offer a honeyed note. Graves, which surround Pessac-Léognan, and Sauterne are the most famous regions for that area. Graves means gravel. The area offers a dry, fresh, crisp white wine, a Sauvignon Blanc, and a Semillon blend. Pessac-Léognan is one of the few areas that age in oak, careful to integrate the fruit and oak. Sauterne is known for its rich, sweet, dessert wine, usually a blend of Sauvignon Blanc and Semillon.

The citrus and acid in white Bordeaux make it a perfect pairing for shellfish, seafood or a cheese soufflé. White wines that are aged in oak can stand up to chicken, duck, pork, and veal.

BURGUNDY

Burgundy lies on the eastern side of France and is known for its Pinot Noir and Chardonnay.

Warm summers and cold winters are perfect for the finicky Pinot Noir grape. The soil in Burgundy is a mix of limestone, clay, gravel, and sand.

When looking for a Pinot Noir in the French wine section on the menu, you might see only one or two that say Pinot Noir in the name, but, if looking at red wine from Burgundy assume they are Pinot Noir. They are well-structured, medium to full-bodied with red fruit, hints of spice, and dark chocolate.

Moving south, the Beaune region is marked by rolling hills and flat open valleys. Pinot Noir dominates in the northern part, but as you head south, Meursault and Chassagne-Montrachet make rich, buttery, bone-dry Chardonnay.

Red Burgundy wines pair well with goat cheese, seared tuna, chicken, lamb, and any white meat, grilled or roasted.

Beaujolais is directly south of Burgundy, part of the Rhône region. The wine is considered to be a young, fruit-forward, light, red wine. Many prefer it a bit chilled. It is 100 percent Gamay, very different from the traditional Burgundy Pinot Noir grape.

A premier white wine, Chablis is the northernmost region in Burgundy. 100 percent Chardonnay marked by crispness and a distinct minerality, with flinty notes from the limestone. Chablis is traditionally aged in stainless steel, keeping it light and crisp. Chardonnay dominates throughout Burgundy.

At the southern end of Burgundy is Mâconnais, a warmer region where Chardonnay is the predominant grape (80 percent). Pouilly Fuissé is probably the most well-known AOC there, producing a crisp, unoaked Chardonnay. Unlike Chablis, Mâconnais Chardonnay is much more powerful, richer, and rounder due to the warmer weather and soil. The classification Macon will always be 100 percent Chardonnay. A California Chardonnay fan might prefer Chardonnay from this region over Chablis because it is bolder and rounder in nature.

White Burgundies' tastes range from fresh peaches to citrus, apple, and honey. They can have a slightly nutty or salty quality and pair well with seafood and white meat, and hold up to a cream sauce and strong cheese.

RHÔNE

Rhône Valley lies in southeastern France. The wines are powerful and full-bodied. There are thirty appellations or AOCs in Rhône. All but Condrieu are known for their full and robust red wines, predominantly Syrah, sometimes mixed with Marsanne and Roussanne (up to 15 percent). They are finely structured with complex aromas, peppery, spicy, smoky, and robust. They include tastes of black cherry, chocolate, licorice, and black pepper. Condrieu specializes in white wines, made almost exclusively from Viognier.

Of thirteen grape varieties approved by AOC laws, the primary indigenous grapes grown in southern Rhône are Syrah, Grenache, Mourvèdre, Viognier, and Roussanne. Warmer, sunnier weather in the south, with breezes off the Mediterranean, make the wines bigger and fuller than Burgundy wines. Grenache is light with flavors of sweet fruit with a hint of spice. The primary grape trio of the region is Grenache, Syrah, and Mourvèdre.

Châteauneuf-du-Pape is one of the most famous southern Rhône wines and is unique in that it has thirteen wine varieties authorized in contributing to its rich, layered taste. Each adds to its unique color, fragrance, and structure. One of my go-to wines at a French restaurant is Gigondas, from just fifteen miles from Châteauneuf-du-Pape. It might not have the same complexity but is usually much more affordable and an incredible crowd-pleaser.

Red Rhône wines go beautifully with any kind of red or white meat, grilled, roasted, braised or stewed. They are wonderful with hearty foods, roast chicken, a classic brie or aged goat cheese. White Rhône wines most widely use Viognier, Marsanne, and Roussanne. They pair well with fish, shellfish, and vegetarian dishes.

LANGUEDOC

Located in southern France, Languedoc is part of the large Mediterranean coastal area now known as the Occitanic region, reaching from the Spanish border in the southeast to the region of Provence in the east. Languedoc makes up 90 percent of the territory, and Roussillon the other 10 percent. Soil types vary with clay and limestone being the most dominant. Schist, shale, granite, pebbles, and sandstone are also throughout the region.

A majority of Languedoc's wines are red blends made with Grenache, Syrah, Carignan, Mourvèdre, and Cinsault, but they also produce rosé, white, and sparkling wines. It is the largest producer of organic wines in France.

The red wines are dominated by cherry and plum when young, and jam, mocha, and spices as they age. It is often associated with an herb blend called garrigue (garig), which is a mix of juniper, rosemary, sage, thyme, and lavender. Grenache is often combined with more tannic grapes, Syrah and Mourvèdre. Syrah with deeply colored red fruit, strong floral notes, a hint of licorice, and spice, is robust with high alcohol and low acid. Mourvèdre is a full-bodied wine, with black fruit, and baking spices with garrigue notes. Carignan has strong tannins, which offer red and black fruit, peppery garrigue, and balsamic notes as it ages. Cinsault is known for its juicy and fruity wines—ruby in color with notes of cranberry and currants. This grape is used in Languedoc's rosé as well as its red blends.

PROVENCE

Provence in the southeastern corner of France, part of the Provence-Alpes-Côte d'Azur is known for its delicious rosé, which is 75 percent of its wine production. The primary grapes used for the production of rosé and red wines are Cinsault, Grenache, Mourvèdre, Syrah, Carignan, Cabernet Sauvignon, and Tibouren.

With mountains, sun, and sea, Provence is picturesque. Its climate is perfect for wine production with mild winters, long hot summers, and a cool breeze off the Mediterranean. The wines are usually full-bodied and fruity, to be drunk young. The seaside towns of Bandol and Cassis overlook the Mediterranean, just east of Marseille. Cassis, one of France's smallest wine regions, is known for its strong, dry white wines made with the Marsanne grape. Bandol is known for its velvety reds, aged in oak, made from the Mourvèdre grape. Bandol also produces white and rosé wines that are crisp, floral, and faintly earthy.

Rosé is made from black (red) grapes. After the grapes are crushed, the skin is left on just long enough to produce a light, pinkish color. Côtes de Provence rosé tend to be dryer and crisper than other rosés. They are fabulous with oysters, scallops, fish, smoked salmon, poultry, cheese soufflés, and vegetable dishes.

CORSICA

Corsica (Island of Beauty) is an island in the Mediterranean Sea, southeast of France and west of Italy. The most notable red grapes are Nielluccio (Sangiovese), known as a rustic, spiced wine of France, and Sciaccarello, a highly fragment grape. Vermentino is a light-bodied white wine similar to a Sauvignon Blanc. I find that those who prefer a Pinot Grigio appreciate a Vermentino.

The elegant fresh and fruity red wines pair well with grilled meats, beef stews, pork chops, sausage, roast squid, and octopus. Vermentino complements fresh herb sauces, pesto, light but rustic cheeses, and shellfish. It makes sense that the wines go with the local cuisine.

Chapter 27

ITALIAN WINES

ITALY, ONE OF THE WORLD'S largest producers of wine, has been making wine for over three thousand years. Although there are more than five hundred different grape varieties and ninety-six provinces, we are going to concentrate on the three major wine regions known for their high-quality table wines: Tuscany (Sangiovese), Piedmont

(Nebbiolo), and Veneto (Corvina). Italy has a DOC classification similar to the AOC in France but theirs includes the aging requirements as well. Italian quality levels are DOCG, DOC, IGT, and Vin da Tavola (VdT or table wines).

TUSCANY (Central Italy)

80 percent of the wines from Tuscany are red.

• **Chianti**—80 percent Sangiovese, 20 percent blend (Cabernet Sauvignon, Merlot, Syrah, etc.) Chianti is dry and savory. It is a medium-bodied wine, tart, and juicy with flavors of cherry with a floral scent. It pairs well with pasta, pizza, meat dishes, and roast chicken.

• **Brunello Di Montalcino**—100 percent Brunello grapes, another name for Sangiovese. A full-bodied wine, with hints of wild berry, licorice, anise, and leather. Many compare it to the Pinot Noir of France as it ages. It pairs with meat dishes, steak, lamb, and grilled game.

• **Vino Nobile di Montepulciano**—70 percent Sangiovese varietal. Dark cherry, plum, oregano, pepper, and tobacco. A rustic wine that softens with age. It pairs with thick meat sauces, veal, mature cheese, and hearty stews.

• **Carmignano**—is a smaller region where DOCG regulates that wines must contain at least 50 percent Sangiovese and 10-20 percent Cabernet Sauvignon or Cabernet Franc plus other indigenous grapes. They are considered a standard Tuscan blend, dry and medium-bodied. They pair well with spicy meats, vegetable dishes, and tomato-based pasta.

• **Bolgheri**—vineyards cover more than two thousand acres. Unlike Brunello and Vino Nobile, these wines can be made with red Bordeaux grapes, Cabernet Sauvignon, Merlot, and Cabernet Franc. They must also add Syrah and Petit Verdot. They have become known as Super Tuscan. They go well with spicy dishes, lasagna, and earthy mushroom dishes.

PIEDMONT (Northwestern Italy)

The two most renowned DOCG wines are Barbaresco and Barolo from the Nebbiolo variety. They have the fullest and most robust style. The soil is rich in lime and clay. The wines are light in color and have a long finish. Barolo is a structured earthy wine, fruit laced with licorice, and coffee notes. It has a fuller finish than Barbaresco. The wines go beautifully with regional foods—braised meets, earthy vegetables, and strong cheeses.

Known primarily for its powerful red wine from the Nebbiolo grape, Piedmont also produces a beautiful white wine, Moscato, and sparkling, Asti Spumante.

Arneis is my favorite white wine from Piedmont and although many are not familiar with it, I suggest seeking it out. It is a fragrant wine with notes of apple and pear and is medium to full-bodied.

VENETO (Northeastern Italy)

This is Italy's largest wine-producing area. White table wines like Orvieto Soave, Pinot Grigio, and Verdicchio. They have citrus notes with a floral bouquet. Through the years winemakers have introduced more international grapes like Chardonnay, Riesling, and Sauvignon Blanc along with the indigenous grapes to make more complex wines for international attraction. In addition to Veneto, some of the best Pinot Grigio come from Friuli and Trentino-Alto Adige, two of the finest growing areas for white wine in Italy.

The more simply produced wines of the region are easy to drink young and fresh. Aged wines are more structured and go beautifully with grilled fish, chicken, and fish-based pasta.

Chapter 28

CALIFORNIA WINES

CALIFORNIA WINEMAKERS HAVE FEW TRADITIONS. They are grounded in modern technology and are much more open to experimenting and blending than the French. It wasn't until the early '70s that the American Viticultural Area (AVA) was established to identify appellation of origin, guaranteeing that a minimum of 85 percent of the wine in the bottle comes from the grapes grown in that appellation. The AVA is similar to the AOC classifications in France (Appellation d'Origine Contrôlée), which was established some thirty years earlier.

REGIONS

North Coast—Napa, Sonoma, Mendocino
* Cabernet Sauvignon, Chardonnay, Merlot, Sauvignon Blanc, Zinfandel

Central Coast (North)—Monterey, Santa Clara, Livermore
* Chardonnay, Grenache, Marsanne, Roussanne, Syrah, Viognier

Central Coast (South)—San Luis Obispo, Santa Barbara, Paso Robles
* Chardonnay, Pinot Noir, Sauvignon Blanc, Syrah

Central Valley—San Joaquin, Sacramento, Fresno, Lodi
* Cabernet Sauvignon, Chardonnay, Chenin Blanc, Colombard, Pinot Noir, Sauvignon Blanc, Syrah, Zinfandel

Although California has over thirty grape varieties, the most prominent reds are Cabernet Sauvignon, Pinot Noir, Zinfandel, Merlot, and Syrah. Cabernet Sauvignon, traditionally from Napa and Sonoma is the most successful grape, the king of the reds, offering a beautiful wine that is full-bodied, dry, ready to drink, and ages gracefully. Pinot Noir from Sonoma, Santa Barbara, and Monterey is a more difficult grape to grow, therefore usually a higher price. Pinot Noir usually has less tannin and matures more quickly than Cabernet, is lighter in body, and is dry. Zinfandel is a beautiful robust wine, accounting for about 10 percent of the wine produced in California. It is a black grape from the North Coast, liken to those in Croatia or Primitivo in Italy. Merlot, like those in France, is round, soft, and silky, making it perfect to blend or have on its own. Syrah, similar to those in southern France, or the Rhône Valley tends to be spicy, robust, and jammy.

When it comes to white wines in California, Chardonnay, Pinot Gris, and Sauvignon Blanc are the three most popular. California Chardonnay makes one think of a full-bodied, buttery wine with a big oak finish. Pinot Gris is refreshing and crisp with hints of lemon, green apple, and honeysuckle. Sauvignon Blanc, the third most popular, like Pinot Gris, is lighter and more acidic than Chardonnay and is herbaceous. Many California wines are fermented in oak barrels. The white wines are dry, with Sauvignon Blanc being just a tad sweeter. When Sauvignon Blanc is aged in oak it takes on a texture as well as creamy, vanilla flavors.

WHITE WINE

Chardonnay—Chardonnay dominates the white wines of the West Coast. It tastes of green apple and citrus. A complex aroma and high acidity deliver a crisp wine. When aged in oak it can offer toasty vanilla and buttery overtones. My recollection is a very full-bodied buttery wine in the '80s and '90s, and now there seems to be a trend for unoaked Chardonnays that highlight the fruit and crispness without the oak influence.

Pinot Gris—a soft, low acidic, slightly aromatic wine. Crisp stone fruit and citrus flavors. Light-bodied.

Sauvignon Blanc—also known as Fume Blanc in California. It is a light, citrus herbaceous wine with fruit flavors of green apple, grapefruit, and melon. Sauvignon Blanc is blended with other varietal wines, especially Semillion, which adds a honeyed note. Crisp, light, fresh, and dry. Medium-bodied.

RED WINE

Cabernet Sauvignon—an opulent, full-bodied, dry, red wine. Fruit-forward with dark fruit, berry, currant, cassis, herbaceous, bell pepper, toasty oak aromas, and earthy flavors.

Merlot—like those in Bordeaux, is a soft and silky wine with plum, dark cherry, and sweet baking spices. It is medium to full-bodied.

Pinot Noir—similar to the French Burgundy's taste of fresh raspberry, plum, and spice. It is light to medium-bodied.

Syrah—blackberry, cassis, black pepper, smoke, dry, dark, and tannic. Similar to the Syrah in Rhône, full-bodied.

Zinfandel—blackberry, cherry, black pepper, anise, and herbs. Medium to full-bodied.

CALIFORNIA SPARKLING WINE

Sparkling wine ranges in style from very dry (natural), and dry (brut) to sweet (sec and demi-sec). A Blanc de Blanc is usually made from the Chardonnay grape and the Blanc de Noirs is from black grapes. Rosé sparkling wines may have a small amount of red wine added to the blend or it may have been allowed brief contact with grape skins for its pale pink finish. Many of the top producers are considered on par with Champagne.

This should give you a good overview of French, Italian, and California wine varieties. As with anything, ask questions, take notes, and seek new opportunities to taste. Take pictures of the labels and write down your thoughts on the wine as well as the price. Find a good local liquor store, ask them questions, and suggestions of some wines for you to taste and compare. Sign up for a wine-tasting class so you can try several wines at one time to compare. Look for restaurants that offer flights or tastings of wine or put together a group and create monthly tastings and enjoy!

PERSONAL NOTE–Schramsberg

I was first introduced to Schramsberg Blanc de Blancs, a Napa sparkling wine in the late '70s. I was taken by the tiny bubbles, beautiful crisp taste, and fabulous packaging. For me, it was near impossible to tell the difference between Schramsberg and Champagne. I hadn't known at that time that Schramsberg Blanc de Blancs was used for the "Toast to Peace" with China's Premier Zhou Enlai and has since been served in the White House by most presidents, if not all.

Schramsberg Vineyard, like many, is stunning. I highly recommend visiting when in Napa. They also have a fantastic website, as does Chandon that not only goes through their history and various wines and winemaking techniques but also offers menu suggestions and recipes. That too is worth a visit.

I served Schramsberg Brut Rosé at my first wedding, thirty-plus years later my friends smile when they see that label. As you find lovely gems that you enjoy and share with others, you too will build memories that will last a lifetime.

Chapter 29

WINE, GRAPES, AND REGIONS
PRONUNCIATION AND DESCRIPTIONS

PROPER PRONUNCIATION IS CRITICAL IN building confidence and making an impression. This section should familiarize you with both the pronunciations and descriptions of wine and their grapes.

Amarone—(Ah·ma·Roh·nay) a red blend from Veneto, Italy, with a rich, strong, and powerful flavor.

Arneis—(ahr·Nayz) Piedmont, Italy, a medium-bodied, fragrant white wine with notes of apple and pear.

Bandol—(ban·doll) an appellation in Provence, France with rich peppery red wines made from Mourvèdre.

Barbaresco—(bar·bah·Res·co) Piedmont, Italy, 100 percent Nebbiolo, fruit laced with licorice, and coffee notes.

Barolo—(Bar·Ro·lo) Piedmont, Italy, 100 percent Nebbiolo. A structured earthy wine, with light fruit, hints of licorice, and coffee. It has a fuller finish than Barbaresco.

Beaujolais—(Boh·jhoe·lay) Rhône, France, 100 percent Gamay, young, light, red fruit, and berry-forward. Some prefer it chilled.

Beaune—(Bone) Southern half of Côte-d'Or in Burgundy known for Pinot Noir and Chardonnay. Reds are fruity with hints of sweet cherry and black currant.

Bordeaux—(bor·Doh) Southwestern part of France known primarily for red wine made from Cabernet Sauvignon, Merlot, and Cabernet Franc.

Brouilly—(Brew·yee) Beaujolais, 100 percent Gamay grape with plum and red fruit, light and full of flavor.

Brunello—(broo·Nehl·oh) Tuscany, Italy, another name for Sangiovese, full-bodied, with hints of wild berry, licorice, anise, and leather.

Burgundy—(Burr·gun·dee) East-central France, known for Pinot Noir and Chardonnay.

Cabernet Franc—(Cab·er·nay fronk) Bordeaux, France, a savory, classic medium-bodied red wine.

Cabernet Sauvignon—(Cab·er·nay Saw·vin·Yawn) full-bodied, rustic, opulent, dry red wine. Fruit-forward with currant, cassis, herbaceous, toasty oak aromas, and earthy flavors.

Carignan—(Care·in·yen) strong tannins that offer red and black fruit, peppery garrigue, and balsamic notes.

Cava—(kaa·vuh) the sparkling wine of Spain, made the same way as Champagne, méthode champenoise, but with grapes that vary by region.

Chablis—(Shab·lee) located just below the Champagne region in France, is 100 percent Chardonnay. It is known for its crispness, distinct minerality, and flinty notes from the limestone.

Champagne—(Sham·payn) located in north-central France, made from Pinot Noir, Chardonnay, and Pinot Meunier. A dry sparkling wine with high acidity, citrus, green fruit flavors, and subtle hints of almond and brioche.

Chardonnay—(shaar·duh·nay) medium to full-bodied, light citrus, varies depending on where it is produced.

Chassagne-Montrachet—(shun·saa·nyuh maan·truch·shay) Côte du Beaune, Burgundy, a rich, buttery, bone-dry Chardonnay.

Chateauneuf-du-Pape—(shah·toh·nuf·doo·pahp) Many say thirteen grape varieties are used to make this powerful, full-bodied red wine from Rhône, France. Grenache is the dominant grape.

Chenin Blanc—(chen·nuhn Blanhn) Loire Valley, France, light white wine with pear, melon, and citrus notes.

Chianti—(kee·yaan·tee) Tuscany, Italy, 80 percent Sangiovese, 20 percent blend (Cabernet Sauvignon, Merlot, Syrah, etc.) a medium-bodied wine, with juicy flavors of cherry and red fruit with floral scent. It can be tart.

Cinsault—(San·soh) part of the southern Rhône blend, juicy and fruity wines—ruby in color with notes of cranberry and currants.

Corvina—(kor·vee·nuh) Veneto, Italy, light to medium bodied, slightly tart with a bitter almond note.

Côtes du Rhône—(koht duh Rohn) basic AOC medium-bodied wines from the Rhône region, Grenache is the primary grape, red fruit, juicy, with hints of cinnamon and spice.

Crémant—(cre·man) a sparkling wine made the same way as Champagne, méthode champenoise, but with grapes synonymous with the region.

Cuvée—(koo·Vay) usually means from the first press of grapes, referencing a higher quality.

Fleurie—(Fluh·ree) Beaujolais, 100 percent Gamay grape, delicate wine with flavors ranging from roses and soft flowers to red fruits and blackberries.

Fumé Blanc—(Foo·may Blahn) California, also known as Sauvignon Blanc. Light, herbaceous wine with fruit flavors of green apple, grapefruit, and melon.

Gamay—(Gam·may) light-bodied, red fruits, strawberry, raspberry, and red cherry. Beaujolais is 100 percent Gamay.

Gewürztraminer—(Guh·Vertz·tra·mean·er) Alsace, full-bodied, aromatic, lychee fruit or tropical fruit and floral notes. Usually off-dry.

Glera—(glare·ah) the grape used in Prosecco.

Grenache—(Gra·Nash) Rhône, France, South of Burgundy, is light with flavors of sweet fruit with a hint of spice.

Languedoc—(lawn·geh·dock) Occitanie (aak·see·tuh·nee) region in southern France, known for Grenache Blanc, Picpoul, Roussanne, Marsanne, Vermentino, and Viognier.

Loire Valley—(luh·waar va·lee) the middle of France, spanning the Loire River. Known for Sancerre, Pouilly-Fumé, and Muscadet.

Macon—(mah·cawn) southern Burgundy, France, 100 percent Chardonnay. It is bolder and rounder than Chablis, with tastes from fresh peaches, citrus, apple, and honey.

Malbec—(mahl·behk) a dark fruit flavor, a bit smoky, heavier wine that is mainly grown in Argentina. Although not discussed in the book, it is one to be familiar with.

Marsanne—(mer·san) a white grape with tastes of orange blossom and baked spices, commonly from northern Rhône.

Merlot—(mehr·loh) Bordeaux, France, a soft and silky, medium to full-bodied wine.

Meursault—(muhr·so) Côte du Beaune, France, rich, buttery, bone-dry Chardonnay.

Mourvèdre—(moor·Veh·drrr) full-bodied wine, with black fruit, and baking spices with garrigue notes.

Muscadet—(Muss·ka·day) Loire Valley, France, Melon de Bourgogne grape, refreshing, citrus, and salty.

Nebbiolo—(Neh·be·oh·low) Piedmont, Italy, big, bold, full-bodied, cherry, rose, leather, and anise notes.

Orvieto Soave—(Or·vee·eh·tow swA·vey) Veneto, Italy, white table wine, citrus notes with a floral bouquet.

Picpoul—(pik·pul) Languedoc region in southern France, a crisp, textured, citrus-scented white wine.

Pinot Grigio—(pee·noe gree·zhee·ow) Veneto, Italy, dry white table wine, citrus notes with a floral bouquet.

Pinot Gris—(pee·noe Gree) Originally from France, cultivated in the Alsace area. Off dry, refreshing, and crisp with hints of lemon, green apple, and honeysuckle.

Pinot Meunier—(pee·noe mun·yay) dark grape used to make Champagne.

Pinot Noir—(pee·noe Nwahr) well-structured, medium to full-bodied, with notes of raspberry, plum, dark chocolate, and spice.

Pouilly Fuissé—(pou·lyi fus·say) crisp, unoaked Chardonnay from the Mâconnais subregion of Burgundy in central France.

Pouilly-Fumé—(pou·yee foo·may) Loire Valley, France, Sauvignon Blanc grape, delicious dry white wine, medium body, stone fruit, and sometimes flinty or smoky notes.

Primitivo—(pri·meh·Tee·voh) Puglia, Italy (the heel of the boot), a deep bold red, fruit-forward, jammy wine, likened to a California Zinfandel.

Prosecco—(proh·sec·koh) Italy's sparkling wine uses the charmat process (large stainless-steel tanks, not individual bottles) with the Glera (glare-ah) grape, with notes of apple, honeysuckle, peach, melon, and pear.

Rhône region—(rown) located in southern France. Many of its wines use Grenache, Syrah, Mourvèdre, Carignan, and Cinsault.

Riesling—(Rees·ling) from Alsace, elegant dry white wines, floral and peachy notes.

Rosé—(roh·Zay) Provence, France is known for their incredible rosé made from Grenache, Cinsault, and Mourvèdre, picked for citrus and tart red fruit flavors. The grapes have limited skin contact for lighter hues.

Roussanne—(roo·Sahn) Rhône region in France, a white grape usually blended with Marsanne. Fuller-bodied, finely structured.

Rully—(rouh·yee) Burgundy, France, produces both Pinot Noir and Chardonnay.

Sancerre—(sahn·Sehr) Loire Valley, France, this Sauvignon Blanc has a stone fruit aroma, lean and vibrant, ripe gooseberry aromas, and fresh-cut grass with a light herbaceous quality.

Sangiovese—(San·joe·Vay·zeh) Tuscany, Italy, medium-bodied, higher acid, dry wine, like a Pinot Noir.

Sauterne—(soh·Tern) rich, sweet, dessert wine, usually a blend of Sauvignon Blanc and Semillon. From the Graves region in Bordeaux.

Sauvignon Blanc—(Soh·vin·yohn Blahnk) stone fruit, hints of white flowers, herbaceous with high acidity.

Semillon—(she·mee·yawn) Bordeaux, France, crisp white, light, fresh, and dry. Medium-bodied, adds a touch of complexity and sometimes a honeyed note.

Syrah—(Sih·Rah) deeply colored red fruit, strong floral notes, robust, a hint of licorice and spice.

Verdicchio—(ver·dee·kee·oh) Veneto, Italy, white table wines, citrus notes with a floral bouquet.

Vermentino—(ver·meh·Tee-noh) Sardinia, Italy, and Corsica, France, white wine with citrus notes.

Viognier—(vee·a·nyay) a medium to full-bodied aromatic white wine from the Languedoc region in southern France.

Vouvray—(Voo·vray) Loire Valley, France, from the Chenin Blanc grape. Flavors of pear, honeysuckle, and apple.

Zinfandel—(Zin·fun·dell) North Coast, California, beautiful robust wine, black grape, liken to those in Croatia or Primitivo in Italy and France. Blackberry, cherry, black pepper, anise, and herbs. Medium to full-bodied.

EPILOGUE

RIGHT AROUND THE TIME I finished an early version of this manuscript, I heard that One Fifth, the restaurant that began my love affair with the restaurant world, would be reopening. I found myself flooded with feelings and memories.

I left One Fifth in 1981, and by the late '80s, the doors shut for good. Many tried to sustain the space, including Anthony Bourdain, but nothing lasted until 2003 when the Batali-Bastianich team opened Otto. Part of their vision was to make it look like an Italian train station with lots of wood, serving high-end pizza and gelato. Otto closed in 2020, as many restaurants did as a result of COVID.

Michelin-star chef Marc Forgione was now set to open a restaurant under its prior name, One Fifth. A very cozy and welcoming space with soft lighting and candles, and a pasta-making station in the front bar room. The walls are lined with vintage pictures and artifacts that pay homage to the building, space, and neighborhood. His menu offers incredible Italian American fare inspired by the Union Square Green Market.

After much contemplation, I found myself walking back through those gold revolving doors. I had never helped open a restaurant before. There were so many people on the first day of training, some curious, some hopeful, and some more knowledgeable about what they were getting into. Opening a new restaurant is a huge undertaking and takes a tremendous commitment from everyone involved.

The FOH training was six hours a day for two weeks, Monday through Friday. We were given manuals on the company, steps of service, multiple menus, food and wine descriptions, allergy sheets, and cocktail ingredients.

Knowing we were responsible for memorizing everything and would be tested verbally, I would go home and create my own spreadsheets, Google ingredients and pronunciations, and then study.

The mornings were for the managers to talk about the company and its philosophy, overall expectations, and the steps of service. We did team-building games and practiced service in the dining room.

It was explained that Chef Marc wants it to be like you are at your grandmother's home for Sunday dinner. The food, prepared as many small plates, comes in a constant flow, just as one thing is finished another magically appears. No need or time to clear the plates, you are there collectively to enjoy the flavors, the food, and the experience. There are no set courses.

This contradicts much of what I have written in this book. The book references a more formal and traditional style and etiquette. But being familiar with the more structured and formal behavior should help you move with purpose and grace in any type of setting.

Although their approach was new to me, it was easier to adapt to once I reminded myself that it wasn't about me, it was about the experience, creating the moment. The challenge was how to present Chef Marc's vision of this shared experience and his amazing cuisine to those who came to the restaurant.

The beverage manager discussed cocktails and wine, and more specifically the twelve wines available by the glass. We were expected to know the producer, grape, region, vintage, and a few descriptors for all twelve as well as the ingredients for the house-made cocktails created by Jeff Bell from Please Don't Tell.

Many did not make it through the first few days. By week two the group was dwindling, so we found ourselves anxiously looking to see who was returning.

In the afternoons, Chef Marc Forgione and Executive Chef Robert Zwirz would present, describe, and discuss the dishes with the staff.

The food was delicate and delicious, and the ingredients were abundant. The number of spices and herbs in each dish was astounding, and the combinations were creative and fantastic. We ate everything we were given and couldn't wait for the next dish to appear. By the end of the training, we would have tasted everything that would be served at One Fifth.

After our two weeks of training and testing, we were ready for what they refer to as a soft open. Friends and family of the chef are invited to sample the menu. Industry people, family, and investors were all on the list. This was to practice service, test our knowledge, and sample the food and cocktails that had been curated for the restaurant to see what tweaks needed to be made before the opening.

On opening night, the entire staff ran outside in front of the entrance for a picture. They had a gigantic red ribbon and three-foot scissors for a ribbon-cutting ceremony—we stopped traffic just for a few minutes. There must have been about fifty of us. It was fantastic. They planned well in advance to create this magical moment.

We went inside for our pre-shift meeting. Chef Marc genuinely and graciously thanked us all for being there and working so hard. He then started with a slow clap as we all joined in, clapping faster and faster until our hands were a flurry, and we couldn't clap any faster. We were all smiling, truly connected. We were a team, ready to open One Fifth.

ADDITIONAL READING SUGGESTIONS

HOSPITALITY

Setting the Table: The Transforming Power of Hospitality in Business by Danny Meyer

Unreasonable Hospitality: The Remarkable Power of Giving People More than They Expect by Will Guidara

ETIQUETTE

Emily Post's Etiquette, The Centennial Edition by Lizzie Post and Daniel Post Senning

Modern Etiquette Made Easy: A Five-Step Method to Mastering Etiquette by Myka Meier

The Mere Mortal's Guide to Fine Dining: From Salad Forks to Sommeliers, How to Eat and Drink in Style Without Fear of Faux Pas by Colleen Rush

WINE

The Essential Wine Book: A Modern Guide to the Changing World of Wine by Zachary Sussman and Editors of PUNCH

The New Wine Rules: A Genuinely Helpful Guide to Everything You Need to Know by Jon Bonné

The Oxford Companion to Wine by Jancis Robinson

The Wine Bible by Karen MacNeil

Windows on the World Complete Wine Course by Kevin Zraly

Wine Folly: Magnum Edition by Madeline Puckette and Justin Hammack

Wine Simple: A Totally Approachable Guide from a World-Class Sommelier by Aldo Sohm and Christine Muhlke

Wine Spectator Magazine, an American lifestyle magazine

COCKTAILS

Death & Co: Modern Classic Cocktails by David Kaplan and Nick Fauchald

Meehan's Bartender Manual: A Cocktail Reference and Recipe Book by Jim Meehan

The Essential Cocktail Book: A Complete Guide to Modern Drinks with 150 Recipes by Editors of PUNCH and Megan Krigbaum

The Joy of Mixology: The Consummate to the Bartender's Craft by Gary Regan

The New Craft of the Cocktail: Everything You Need to Know to Think Like a Master Mixologist, with 500 Recipes by Dale DeGroff and Daniel Krieger

CHEESE

Cheese Primer by Steven Jenkins

The Cheese Course by Janet Fletcher

FUN READ

Live! From Tribeca, by Frank Digiacomo, September 2008, Vanity Fair https://www.vanityfair.com/style/2005/11/odeon200511

Acknowledgements

THIS BOOK WAS MADE POSSIBLE in large part due to my wonderful memories with my incredible friends and business associates: Suzanne Bronski, Joanne Cini, Cheryl Cox, Delia Delisser, Susan Levin, Monty Jackson, Samantha Robinson, Bob Sacha, Regina Schrambling, Donna Rude Slight, Michael Uslan, Kendra Epstein, Wally Konrad, Lisa MacLaughlin, Cathy Mullen, Cynthia Pierce, Jen Schoon, Rick McGuire, Rudy Taylor, Dan Carlin, Kate Kelleher, Gail Yancosek, Nick Gardner, Amy Bergen, Malachy Williams, Joan Zidow, Janet Canata, Louise Coccaro, Lorraine Cooper, Meg Courtney, Jo Engle, Bob Hesse, Alan Straub, Karl Wexler, Judi Wojciechowski, Jane Zonino-Gresham, Randy Altman, Marjorie Auster, Connie Betro, Andrea Blum, Joan DiCarlo, Palma D'Orazio, Rosalie Ehrenberg, Steve Eisenberg, Danielle Ferdinand, Gwen Flemming, Geraldine Gately, Anne Goldberg, Peggy Green, Jim Hyde, Patrice Kawas, Lisa Kleinman, Elaine Levine, Lois Levine, Eileen Lieboff, Nina Lloyd, Bob Lynch, Nancy Petrino, Jennifer Renda, Chris Rios, Pam Rosenberg, Marcy Sackett, Nancy Samuels, Lisa Sangalli, Liz Seif-Gore, Scott Semaya, Allison Shapiro, Florence Spina, Jane Townsend, Diane Werner, Mark Hertenstein, and my mom, Angela Teichmann. Thank you for all the beautiful meals and experiences over the years.

Thank you to my amazing daughter and favorite dining

partner, Emily Robinson, whose constant support, notes, restaurant suggestions, and dining experiences were invaluable.

To my wonderful publisher, Cheryl Benton, amazing proofreader, Anne Marie Rutella, talented book designer, Susan Herbst, and very creative illustrator, Lana Lê, a special thanks for your patience, guidance, and expertise.

And much thanks and gratitude to restaurant-world legends: George Schwarz, Kiki Kogelnik, Keith McNally, Phil Nugent, Michael Finney, Frank Ventura, Tony Cheng, Roberta Rossini Delice, Chef Marcus Glocker, Lorraine Chevallier, Brandon Fults, Robert Khimeche, Zouheir Louhaichy, Chef Marc Forgione, Chef Robert Zwirz, Tommy Hart, Dennis Martin, Pat Brennen, Michael Feherty, Timmy Butler, and Paddy Ford all of whom made me love and appreciate restaurants, food, and the dining experience. I am in awe of the passion and creativity that they bring to the experience every day, and thankful I was there to learn, join in, and enjoy.

About The Author

DEBBIE VON AHRENS IS EXCITED TO share her passion for restaurants and hospitality through business executives' eyes in her debut book *The Business of Dining: A Guide to Making a Five-Star Impression.*

With a rich background in the culinary world, Debbie's journey has taken her through some of New York City's most renowned restaurants, including Balthazar, Augustine, and One Fifth. Her experience as V.P. Director of Sales for FOX5 New York, and UPN9 allowed her to entertain clients in top-notch restaurants and venues across the country.

Debbie's passion for understanding the intricacies of business, coupled with her love for fine dining and the arts, has driven her to excel academically as well. She holds a Bachelor of Science degree from NYU in Marketing and Economics, which has undoubtedly contributed to her multifaceted success.

Residing in the vibrant city of New York, Debbie continues to be an influential figure in the culinary and entertainment scenes. With her debut book, *The Business of Dining*, readers can expect to gain invaluable insights into creating a five-star impression, making this an essential guide for both aspiring entrepreneurs and seasoned professionals.

Quick Reference Index

CONVERSATION, WAITERS, AND GOOD GUESTS

PAYING THE BILL

MENUS

ALLERGIES

FOOD

COCKTAILS

PEOPLE AND PLACES

www.ingramcontent.com/pod-product-compliance
Lightning Source LLC
Chambersburg PA
CBHW070708130626
46553CB00005B/1895